Study Guide

International Economics
Ninth Edition

Robert J. Carbaugh
Central Washington University

Prepared by

James S. Hanson
Willamette University

THOMSON

SOUTH-WESTERN

Australia · Canada · Mexico · Singapore · Spain · United Kingdom · United States

THOMSON

SOUTH-WESTERN

Study Guide (prepared by James S. Hanson)

to accompany

International Economics, 9e (by Robert J. Carbaugh)

Vice President/Editorial Director:
Jack Calhoun

Vice President/Editor-in-Chief:
Michael P. Roche

Publisher of Economics:
Michael B. Mercier

Acquisitions Editor:
Michael Worls

Developmental Editor:
Andrew McGuire

Sr. Production Editor:
Elizabeth A. Shipp

Sr. Marketing Manager:
Janet Hennies

Media Developmental Editor:
Peggy Buskey

Media Production Editor:
Pam Wallace

Manufacturing Coordinator:
Sandee Milewski

Sr. Design Project Manager:
Michelle Kunkler

Cover Designer:
Beckmeyer Design/Cincinnati, Ohio

Cover Images:
© PhotoDisc, Inc.

Printer:
Victor Graphics, Inc.

Table of Contents

Preface

I have prepared this study guide and workbook because of my conviction that students will learn and become excited about international economics primarily through active involvement. My own students have strengthened their grasp of theory and policy applications by working through the questions and problems in the study guide, and have contributed to stimulating class discussion through oral reports based on the "explorations beyond the classroom" suggestions at the end of each chapter. I hope that students will find this new edition equally beneficial.

I would like to thank Robert Carbaugh for his continuing support and valuable advice on this project. I also have appreciated the support of Andrew McGuire at South-Western Publishing Company, and the many helpful suggestions provided by an anonymous copyeditor. I am indebted to former and current international economics students at Willamette University for helpful comments on earlier drafts. It is primarily because of their suggestions that I have added and then expanded a section at the end of the study guide with answers to many of the problems and short answer questions. I remain thankful to Karmen Cates for her skillful editorial and formatting assistance initially with this project, to Robin Chung for her computer graphics work, and to Corina Mallory for her careful editorial and proofing assistance. I am indebted to Jesse Mar-Chun for his extensive graphics work and formatting assistance on the previous edition, and to Jeff Deeder for his assistance with this revision.

I look forward to suggestions for continued improvements, and welcome comments and questions from faculty and students who are using this study guide and workbook.

James S. Hanson
Professor of Economics
Willamette University
Salem, OR 97301

Phone: (503) 370-6316

E-mail: jhanson@willamette.edu

CHAPTER 1

THE INTERNATIONAL ECONOMY

INTRODUCTION TO STUDY GUIDE AND WORKBOOK

SYNOPSIS OF CHAPTER CONTENT

International economics deals with economic relations in a global economy characterized by increasing interdependence among nations. One component of such interdependence is the trading relations among nations, through exports and imports of goods and services. Such trade involves manufactured products, but also exports and imports of energy and other raw materials, some of which are becoming increasingly scarce. Other dimensions of interdependence include economic aid from one nation to another, and loans, which have created serious problems of foreign debt for some nations. Short-term capital flows among nations with increasing ease, as investors seek high interest rates and safe havens. Multinational enterprises establish operations around the world, including a growing presence of foreign multinationals in the United States, making it increasingly difficult to determine whether IBM, with nearly half of its operations outside the United States, or Toyota, with auto factories in Kentucky, is the more "American" company.

This book begins with a focus on why nations choose to trade with each other, and why they often adopt trade or commercial policies that include tariffs and other trade barriers rather than adopting completely free trade policies. Trade policies of developing countries, regional trade agreements, and the movements of capital and labor among countries also are examined in the first major section of the text, comprising Chapters 2 through 10. Beginning with Chapter 11, our focus shifts to the monetary or financial side of international economics, dealing with the balance of payments, foreign exchange markets, international banking activities, and changes in the international monetary system through which nations attempt to manage their financial relations with each other.

This study guide and workbook is designed to supplement the primary text. The first segment of each chapter provides a brief summary of the main points in the corresponding text chapter. The remaining components of each study guide chapter are outlined briefly below. They reflect the author's strong conviction that students learn international economics most effectively by becoming actively involved with the material, by "doing" the economics rather than simply reading about it. Thus, students are encouraged to use this guide as a genuine "workbook," taking pen or pencil in hand, working individually or in small groups to answer the questions posed and problems presented, mastering the theory and grappling enthusiastically with the important policy issues found in the real world of international economics.

KEY CONCEPTS AND TERMS

This section is designed to help solidify your grasp of the important economic concepts presented in each chapter. Try not only to define each term, but also to illustrate its significance in regard to your understanding of international economic relations.

TRUE OR FALSE?

These questions are designed not so much to test your memorization of facts as to challenge you to think analytically about international economic theory and policy. Try to think through this analysis, and perhaps explain your reasoning to other students, rather than simply identifying the correct response.

MULTIPLE CHOICE

The multiple choice questions also are designed to give you practice in using economic analysis to understand theoretical relationships and policy issues. Again, try to explain the reasoning behind your selections.

PROBLEMS AND SHORT ANSWER QUESTIONS

This component gives you the greatest opportunity to "do" international economics. Challenge yourself not only to "think" about the questions but actually to write out responses to the short essay questions and to work through or solve the problems presented. This is perhaps the best way to increase your mastery of and self-confidence regarding international economics, and to prepare for class discussions and examinations. Working in small groups to answer these questions and to review your answers can be very helpful.

EXPLORATIONS BEYOND THE CLASSROOM

This final segment of each chapter is designed to move students beyond the text and the classroom into the real world of international economics. The goal is to find examples in current publications that illustrate the relevance of concepts and theories developed in the text. These questions provide good opportunities for students to bring to life what they have learned from the text. An effective way to enhance your participation in class is to select one of these questions and work with a small group of two or three students to do some brief library research and prepare a short oral class presentation on your findings.

SUPPLEMENTARY REFERENCES (These resources may be helpful in connection with the "Explorations Beyond the Classroom" questions.)

Encyclopedias, Dictionaries

> Encyclopedia of Economics
> International Encyclopedia of the Social Sciences
> The New Palgrave: A Dictionary of Economics

Newspapers

> The Christian Science Monitor
> The New York Times
> The Wall Street Journal
> Newsletters issued by Federal Reserve district banks and by major commercial banks such as Citibank, Chase Manhattan, and J.P. Morgan

Magazines, Reports on International Economic Policy

> Business Week
> Challenge
> Congressional Quarterly Weekly Report. U.S. Congress
> The Economist (London)
> Fortune
> Far Eastern Economic Review
> U.N. Chronicle
> U.N. Observer

Sources of Data and International Statistics

Balance of Payments Statistics. International Monetary Fund
Direction of Trade Statistics. International Monetary Fund
Economic Report of the President. President of the United States
The Europa World Yearbook. London
Federal Reserve Bulletin. Board of Governors of the U.S. Federal Reserve System
International Financial Statistics Yearbook. International Monetary Fund
International Trade (annual). General Agreement on Tariffs and Trade
International Trade Statistics Yearbook. United Nations
Survey of Current Business. U.S. Department of Commerce
World Development Report. The World Bank
World Economic Survey. United Nations

Sources of Information on the Internet

CNN Interactive (international news).
    http://www.cnn.com/
U.S. Department of Commerce. International Trade Administration.
    http://www.ita.doc.gov/
U.S. Department of the Treasury. United States Customs Service.
    http://www.customs.treas.gov
U.S. International Trade Commission.
    http://www.usitc.gov/
United States Trade Representative.
    http://www.ustr.gov/
Export-Import Bank of the United States.
    http://www.exim.gov/
U.S. Federal Reserve System.
    http://www.bog.frb.fed.us/
U.S. Agency for International Development.
    http://www.info.usaid.gov/
International Monetary Fund.
    http://www.imf.org/
World Trade Organization.
    http://www.wto.org/
World Bank.
    http://www.worldbank.org/
United Nations.
    http://www.un.org/
Organization for Economic Co-operation and Development.
    http://www.oecd.fr/
Inter-American Development Bank.
    http://www.iadb.org/
OANDA: Currency Converter (foreign exchange rates).
    http://www.oanda.com

3

CHAPTER 2

FOUNDATIONS OF MODERN TRADE THEORY

SYNOPSIS OF CHAPTER CONTENT

This chapter focuses on why nations trade with each other, how we determine the gains or benefits to nations from trade, and which factors influence the pattern of each nation's exports and imports.

Beginning in the early 1500s with the period of nation building in Europe, a group known as the **mercantilists** emphasized the benefits to a nation from generating a trade surplus. Such a surplus, an excess of exports over imports, would lead to payments in gold or silver by other nations in order to finance their corresponding trade deficits. These revenues would enable governments to increase domestic spending and output, and also to finance armies committed to defending or expanding national borders or spheres of influence. This perspective reflects a "zero-sum game" view of international trade, with surplus nations gaining at the expense of deficit nations.

David Hume developed a **price-specie-flow doctrine** to show that national use of trade barriers to achieve such trade surpluses would be self-defeating, since the revenue inflows would soon raise domestic price levels, making the nation's exports less competitive and eventually converting the trade surplus into a balanced trade position.

With the publication of Adam Smith's famous *Wealth of Nations* in 1776, the perspective shifted to a "positive-sum game" view of trade, recognizing that trade enables all participating nations to benefit from higher consumption levels. In Smith's model, labor productivities differ from one nation to another. Each nation specializes in producing that item in which it has an **absolute advantage** based on lower labor costs, exporting some of this output in order to import at a lower opportunity cost those items in which other nations have absolute advantages. Such international division of labor according to absolute advantage enables each nation to benefit from lower-cost imports. This result led Smith to advocate policies of free trade to secure such benefits, rather than the restrictive trade policies favored by the mercantilists in order to achieve trade surpluses. An essential insight of Smith's theory is that the gains from trade are consumption benefits in the form of low-cost imports, with exports representing the cost of acquiring such imports rather than something to be valued in themselves as contributing to a trade surplus.

David Ricardo went beyond Adam Smith's analysis to develop the **principle of comparative advantage**, again using a model based on labor productivity. Ricardo's model, however, showed that even a nation that is absolutely less efficient in producing all products can gain by exporting the product in which its absolute disadvantage is least; even the nation with an absolute advantage in all products can gain from importing that product in which its absolute advantage is proportionately least. Stated differently, each nation exports that product in which it has a comparative advantage, and imports that product in which it has a comparative disadvantage. Thus, in a simple two-country, two-product model, a nation with absolute cost disadvantages in both products still can compete effectively in international trade by exporting that product in which it has a comparative advantage. Both nations will benefit by importing those products that can be produced abroad comparatively more efficiently than at home.

The benefits from specialization according to comparative advantage can be demonstrated in examples where nations trade on a barter basis, for instance exchanging bottles of wine for yards of cloth. Without trade, the **barter exchange rate** between wine and cloth in each country reflects the relative productivity of labor in producing wine versus cloth in that country. Wine will be relatively less expensive (in terms of yards of cloth) in that country whose labor productivity gives it a comparative advantage in producing wine. A barter exchange rate between those that would prevail in each country without trade will create an incentive for each country to specialize in production according to its own comparative advantage, and to import from the other country that product in which it has a comparative disadvantage.

In the real world, most of us deal with prices in money rather than barter terms. Simple examples can be modified to show how differing labor productivities will be reflected in relative prices in each country without trade (for instance, the dollar price of a bottle of wine relative to the dollar price of a yard of cloth). Then, in an example involving the United States and the United Kingdom, one can show that for a given set of dollar prices in the United States and pound prices in the United Kingdom, the exchange rate between the dollar and the pound must fall within a certain range in order for trade and specialization according to comparative advantage to appear profitable within each country.

Even such simple models, although static in nature, can be made more dynamic by showing how changing labor productivities over a period of time can eliminate a nation's historical comparative advantage in a particular product or create a new set of comparative advantages among nations, contributing to dramatic changes in trade patterns over time. This also helps to bring out the importance of national government policies as they affect labor productivity and either enhance or alter each nation's comparative advantage in a dynamic context. Incorporating money prices also makes it possible to show how more rapid inflation in one country than in another eventually can price that nation's export products out of the market if the exchange rate does not adjust to reflect this difference in relative inflation rates.

Ricardo's simple model of comparative advantage, because it is based on constant opportunity costs, leads to **complete specialization**, with each nation producing only that product in which it has a comparative advantage and importing all that it consumes of the other product. The vulnerability that this implies might lead nations to use import barriers to preserve domestic production in critical sectors such as agriculture and national defense.

A somewhat more realistic view of international trade emerges when we recognize that the opportunity cost of producing a good is not constant as in the Smith and Ricardo models, but rather increases as more of a particular good is produced. In an example with wheat and auto production, increasing costs would result because resources more suited to wheat production and less suited to auto production would be reallocated as a nation shifted from an emphasis on wheat to a greater emphasis on auto production. The principle of **diminishing marginal productivity** also helps explain the rising unit production costs as more autos are produced.

With increasing costs, a nation's **transformation schedule**, showing the production possibilities for wheat and autos, becomes bowed out, in contrast to the straight-line transformation schedules of the Smith and Ricardo models. Thus, the **marginal rate of transformation** (MRT), representing each nation's ability to shift from wheat to auto production, is reflected in the slope of the transformation schedule and thus changes from one point to another along this schedule.

For example, if Canada has a comparative advantage in wheat and the United State in autos, the MRT initially will be steeper for Canada than for the United States, reflecting the higher relative cost of autos in Canada. As trade takes place and specialization begins, the MRT will become flatter for Canada as it moves toward more wheat production, reflecting the increasing relative cost of producing wheat. The MRT for the United States will become steeper with a shift toward more auto production, reflecting the increasing relative cost of producing autos as resources are reallocated from wheat to auto production. For free and balanced trade, the MRT must be the same in Canada as in the United States, and the amount of wheat that Canada wishes to export in exchange for auto imports must equal the amount of wheat that the United States wishes to import. Such an MRT must have a slope somewhere between the initial relatively steep MRT of Canada and the relatively flat MRT of the United States.

A fundamental insight of this more realistic model is that trade leads only to **incomplete specialization**, with each nation continuing to produce some of the product that it imports. For instance, even though wheat becomes relatively more expensive in Canada as the slope of Canada's MRT decreases, the increasing relative cost of wheat production causes firms to reach a point where shifting further resources from auto to wheat production would not be profitable. Similarly, as autos become more expensive in the United States and more autos are produced, firms reach a point where the increasing relative cost of auto production makes a further shifting of resources from wheat to auto production unprofitable. Each nation thus continues to produce some of its import product as it moves toward greater specialization in production for export according to comparative advantage.

The gains from trade take the same form here as in the simpler Ricardian model. Each nation, by specializing in production according to its comparative advantage, is enabled to consume beyond its transformation schedule, potentially consuming both more wheat and more autos than the limits of its own internal production possibilities would permit. The **trade triangle**, connecting each nation's production and consumption points after trade takes place, no longer appears at a corner of the nation's transformation schedule as in the Ricardian model, where each nation specializes completely and where its imports and its consumption of the import product are equivalent. Rather, with increasing costs each nation specializes only incompletely, so the trade triangle originates at an interior point along its transformation schedule and shows that each nation's imports will equal the difference between what it consumes of its import good and what it produces of that item. As before, the trade triangle shows each nation's exports to equal the difference between how much it produces of its comparative advantage product and how much of that item it chooses to consume.

These simple two-country, two-product models of international trade can be extended to include a large number of products, so that for each country many products can be arranged along a spectrum according to degree of comparative cost. The point along this spectrum separating export from import products depends on relative costs and relative strengths of demand in each country. Similarly, more than two countries can be incorporated; each country continues to export according to its comparative advantage, but more complex triangular or multilateral trading relationships among countries emerge. Thus a nation might export to another nation but import nothing from that particular nation, and trade balance requires only that each nation's global imports and exports be equal, not that it have a "bilateral" trade balance with each trading partner. This point has particular practical significance in light of the current policy focus on the bilateral trade balance between Japan and the United States.

How realistic are these relatively simple comparative advantage models? Several empirical studies have found that export and import trade patterns among nations do correlate well with relative labor productivities, with each nation tending to export those products in which it has relatively high labor productivity. However, the Ricardian model has severe limitations because of its assumption that labor is the only input to production, and extensions to incorporate other relevant factors are required in order to achieve greater realism and predictability.

KEY CONCEPTS AND TERMS (Define each concept, and briefly explain its significance.)

Mercantilism

Price-specie-flow mechanism

Absolute advantage

Comparative advantage

Labor theory of value

Complete specialization

Gains from international trade

Terms of trade, barter exchange rate

Transformation schedule, or production possibilities frontier

Marginal rate of transformation

Increasing opportunity costs, diminishing marginal productivity

Partial or incomplete specialization

Trade triangle

TRUE OR FALSE? (On an exam, be prepared to explain *why* the statement is true or false.)

T F 1. Mercantilists believed that each nation should try to achieve balanced trade, with exports equal to imports.

T F 2. Hume's price-specie-flow doctrine explained why nations would not be able continually to increase their gold holdings through ongoing trade surpluses.

T F 3. Adam Smith believed that the wealth of nations was established primarily through exports used to purchase gold and silver rather than imports.

T F 4. Smith's absolute advantage theory showed that two nations could both gain from trade by exporting products in which their labor productivity was higher than that of the other nation.

T F 5. Ricardo's principle of comparative advantage showed that nations could gain through trade by specializing in production according to comparative advantage, even if one nation had an absolute cost advantage in all products.

T F 6. The transformation schedule for Ricardo's comparative advantage model is bowed out, rather than straight.

T F 7. In Ricardo's comparative model, trade results in complete specialization.

T F 8. With increasing costs or diminishing marginal productivity, the opportunity cost of each nation's export product goes down as it specializes more in production for export.

T F 9. The gains from trade show that each nation can consume more of its import product only by consuming less of its export product than it did before beginning to trade.

T F 10. The principle of comparative advantage applies only in simple two-country models, not in the real world where many countries trade with each other.

MULTIPLE CHOICE

1. In Smith's absolute advantage theory of trade,
   a. a country with the absolute advantage in all products eventually will acquire all the gold and silver
   b. a country with the absolute advantage will have a large trade surplus
   c. both countries will gain from trade if each exports that product for which it has lower labor costs
   d. a country will lose its absolute advantage if it does not protect its industry with tariff barriers

2. David Hume's price-specie-flow doctrine demonstrates that
   a. the primary goal of trade is to maintain large trade surpluses in order to acquire gold and silver
   b. international trade is a "zero-sum game"
   c. mercantilist policies will create large gains from trade
   d. trade surpluses and the resulting revenue inflows will cause domestic prices to rise, making the trade surpluses temporary rather than permanent

3. Ricardo's principle of comparative advantage shows that
   a. trade leads to incomplete specialization
   b. even a country with no absolute cost advantage can gain from trade by exporting that product in which its absolute cost disadvantage is relatively least
   c. countries with absolute cost advantages will gain more from trade than will those without such cost advantages
   d. only countries with comparative advantages will be able to achieve trade surpluses

4. If each worker in Argentina can produce either 3 bushels of wheat or 1 auto, and each worker in Brazil can produce either 4 bushels of wheat or 2 autos,
   a. Brazil has an absolute advantage in wheat and autos, and Argentina has no comparative advantage
   b. Argentina has an absolute advantage in wheat and autos, and Brazil has no comparative advantage
   c. Brazil has an absolute advantage in wheat and autos, but Argentina has a comparative advantage in autos
   d. Brazil has an absolute advantage in wheat and autos, but Argentina has a comparative advantage in wheat

5. In Question 4, a barter exchange rate that would bring about mutually beneficial trade between Argentina and Brazil is
   a. 3 bushels of wheat for 1 auto
   b. 4 bushels of wheat for 2 autos
   c. 5 bushels of wheat for 2 autos
   d. 3 bushels of wheat for 2 autos

6. A central policy lesson of the principle of comparative advantage is that a nation gains from international trade
   a. by generating large export surpluses
   b. by gaining access to imports at lower opportunity costs than if it produced those goods domestically
   c. if it is larger than its trading partners
   d. if it is absolutely more efficient than its trading partners

7. With increasing rather than constant opportunity costs, trade between nations results in
   a. complete specialization and falling production costs within each nation
   b. incomplete specialization, with unchanging production costs for exports within each nation
   c. incomplete specialization, with the opportunity cost of producing exports rising within each nation
   d. incomplete specialization, with the opportunity cost of producing exports falling within each nation

8. When a nation begins to trade according to comparative advantage rather than remaining self sufficient,
   a. the price of its export product rises relative to the price of its import product
   b. the price of its export product falls relative to the price of its import product
   c. its production possibilities schedule shifts outward
   d. its gold reserves will increase

9. The simple two-country, two-product models of international trade presented in most textbooks
    a. can be extended to include more countries but not more products
    b. can be extended to include more products but not more countries
    c. can be extended to include many countries and products, with each pair of countries having bilateral trade balances
    d. can be extended to include many countries and products, with each country having balanced trade but not necessarily with any single trading partner

10. Empirical studies of actual international trade patterns
    a. support the absolute advantage theory of Adam Smith
    b. are fully consistent with Ricardo's comparative advantage theory
    c. provide partial support for Ricardo, but find his labor theory of value to have severe limitations
    d. find that trade patterns do not correlate in any way with relative labor productivities, as predicted by Ricardo

PROBLEMS AND SHORT ANSWER QUESTIONS

1. Use the following example to illustrate Adam Smith's principle of absolute advantage in international trade. Construct transformation or production possibilities frontiers for each country, identify each country's absolute advantage, determine a barter exchange rate that would lead to mutually beneficial trade, construct the trading line for each country to reflect this barter exchange rate, and illustrate potential trade triangles for each country.

	Argentina	Brazil
Output per worker		
Wheat	3	2
Autos	1	2
Total labor supply	12	12

2. Use the following example to illustrate David Ricardo's principle of comparative advantage, repeating each step of the process outlined in Question 1. Explain also how both countries can gain from trade, even though Brazil has the absolute advantage in both wheat and autos.

	Argentina	Brazil
Output per worker		
Wheat	3	4
Autos	1	2
Total labor supply	12	12

3. Construct a table showing feasible choices for consumption of wheat and autos in Argentina and in Brazil before trade, and use this table also to show how specialization according to comparative advantage would enable each nation to consume both more wheat and more autos than was possible without trade. [*Hint*: Use the terms of trade that you selected to represent the gains from trade in Question 2 to determine the amount of imports which each nation could acquire for a given level of exports.]

4. Use the graphs that you constructed in Question 2 to show how the comparative advantages of each nation could be reversed if training and education in Argentina dramatically improved its labor productivity in auto production over a 10-year period.

5.	Show how the economic gains from trade would be reduced if Argentina decided to use an import quota to protect its auto industry from falling below an output level of 2 cars per year.

6.	Use the following pair of examples to illustrate Ricardo's principle of comparative advantage, repeating each step of the process outlined in Question 1.

    a.	In England, 6 units of labor are required to produce 1 unit of food, while it takes 8 units of labor to produce 1 unit of clothing. Germany can produce 1 unit of food with 2 units of labor and can produce 1 unit of clothing with 4 units of labor. Each country has 48 units of labor available. Which country has the comparative advantage in food? Which country has the comparative advantage in clothing? Give an example of a barter exchange rate between food and clothing that would bring about mutually beneficial trade between England and Germany.

    b.	In England, 1 unit of labor can produce 1/6 unit of food or 1/8 unit of clothing. In Germany 1 unit of labor can produce 1/2 unit of food or 1/4 unit of clothing. Each country has 48 units of labor available. Which country has the comparative advantage in food? Which country has the comparative advantage in clothing? Give an example of a barter exchange rate between food and clothing that would bring about mutually beneficial trade between England and Germany.

Explain why this pair of examples actually represents two different ways of presenting the same information, leading to identical results.

7.   Suppose that the curves below represent the transformation or production possibilities for Argentina and Brazil.

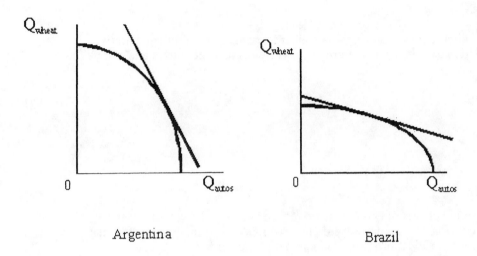

Argentina   Brazil

a.   Explain how these curves reflect increasing rather than constant cost conditions. Why is this likely to occur in the real world?

b.   Why is the barter exchange rate between wheat and autos steeper for Argentina than for Brazil? How does this reflect different relative opportunity costs in the two countries?

c.   Draw a new terms-of-trade or barter exchange rate line for each country that would represent the potential for mutually beneficial trade. Why must this line have the same slope for both countries?

13

d. Explain why this terms-of-trade line leads each country to specialize only incompletely according to its comparative advantage. Draw potential trade triangles for each country to illustrate the potential gains from trade. Why must these triangles be the same size for both countries if trade balance is to occur?

8. Explain verbally how the simple two-country, two-product Ricardian model of comparative advantage can be extended to explore trade patterns in a world of many countries and many different products.

9. How successful have been the efforts of economists to test empirically the validity of the Ricardian model in the real world? In what ways do the assumptions of this model (for instance, that labor is the only factor of production) limit its explanatory power?

EXPLORATIONS BEYOND THE CLASSROOM

1. Search for newspaper or magazine articles that discuss recent developments in a particular nation's export performance, focusing particularly on major export products. What insights can you draw regarding this nation's comparative advantage in international trade?

2. What evidence can you find in recent news articles regarding strategies used by specific countries to strengthen their existing comparative advantages or to develop new comparative advantages in trade?

3. Select a country that has experienced significant economic growth and development over the past 10 or 15 years. Use publications of the International Monetary Fund to explore how this country's current pattern of exports and imports differs from what it was earlier. How does this illustrate significant changes over time in this nation's comparative advantage?

CHAPTER 3

INTERNATIONAL EQUILIBRIUM

SYNOPSIS OF CHAPTER CONTENT

Comparative advantage theory focuses on supply characteristics within each country to explain the basis for specialization and the gains to each country from international trade. This chapter extends that analysis to show how demand considerations enter into the determination of international trade patterns and the gains from trade.

To illustrate the role of tastes and preferences for products within each country, the economist introduces the **indifference curve** concept. In a simple two-product model, a single indifference curve for an individual represents various combinations of goods (e.g., autos and bushels of wheat) that are of equal value to that person. Such a curve is negatively sloped, indicating a willingness to give up some wheat in exchange for more autos. Moreover, the slope changes along an indifference curve, because each time wheat is exchanged for more autos, the value of the next bushel of wheat given up becomes greater and the value of the next auto acquired becomes less. Thus, the indifference curve is bowed in or convex to the diagram's origin. The absolute value of the indifference curve's slope is called the **marginal rate of substitution** (MRS), because it represents the willingness of the individual to substitute autos for wheat at each point along the indifference curve.

Since an individual is assumed to derive more satisfaction from additional wheat or additional autos, increasing the amount of one without changing the amount of the other will provide greater total satisfaction, placing the individual on a higher indifference curve. Thus, each person has not just one indifference curve but an entire "family" or set of curves, together constituting an indifference map. Although our ability to go from the values or preferences of an individual to those of a group of people is severely limited, in order to analyze international trade patterns economists often work with indifference maps as if they represent the collective preferences of all people within a given nation.

Superimposing such a national or community indifference map on the production frontier, or transformation schedule, for that nation enables us to see how that nation would best utilize its resources if it were self-sufficient and did not trade. The highest indifference curve attainable is the one that is just tangent to the transformation schedule, and this tangency point indicates the optimal combination of wheat and autos for that nation to produce and consume. The slope of the tangent to the indifference curve and the transformation schedule at this point reflects the marginal rate of substitution between wheat and autos at this point of maximum satisfaction.

In order to see the potential for gains from international trade, the slope of this tangent line also can be interpreted as the **terms of trade**, or the rate at which the nation can exchange wheat for autos in international trade. For instance, a steeper terms-of-trade line (reflecting more wheat exchanged for a given number of autos) would induce the nation to shift toward more auto production and less wheat production, reaching a new tangency point of this line with its steeper terms-of-trade line. In effect, the higher value of autos relative to wheat encourages firms to expand auto production and contract wheat production. At the same time, there will be another tangency point of this steeper terms-of-trade line with a higher indifference curve than was attainable without trade. This point represents the optimal consumption point, the best combination of wheat and auto consumption that this nation can realize through domestic production and international trade. Because at this point the nation would be consuming more wheat than it produced, and fewer autos than it produced, it would be exporting autos and importing wheat, as can be seen by comparing the production and consumption points. The national gains from production specialization and international trade are represented by this movement from a lower to a higher indifference curve in the consumption of wheat and autos.

In a similar manner, a flatter terms-of-trade line (reflecting less wheat exchanged for a given number of autos) would induce the nation to shift toward more wheat and less auto production, and to shift its consumption through trade to a new tangency point on a higher indifference curve, in this case consuming more autos than it produced and exporting wheat for imports of autos. Again, this movement to a higher indifference curve represents the gains from trade.

In the Ricardian theory, supply conditions determined that the domestic price line (reflecting the amount of wheat exchanged for a given number of autos) without trade would be steeper for a country with a comparative advantage in wheat than for a country with a comparative advantage in autos. The terms-of-trade line with international trade would fall between these two extremes; it would be flatter than the domestic price line for the first country, inducing it to produce wheat for export in exchange for greater numbers of autos than before trade, and it would be steeper than the domestic price line for the second country, enabling it to purchase more imported wheat for a given number of autos than it could produce internally. The Ricardian analysis was unable to specify the exact position of the terms-of-trade line between these limits, however.

Incorporating the demand side into the analysis enables us to complete this picture, as demonstrated by John Stuart Mill in his **theory of reciprocal demand**. In effect, Mill showed that a country's desire to trade at a given terms of trade would be determined by comparing its optimal production point (the tangency point of the terms-of-trade line with that country's transformation schedule) and its optimal consumption point (the tangency point of the terms-of-trade line with that country's highest attainable indifference curve). If demand patterns (indifference curves) are similar in the two countries, the different pre-trade domestic price line slopes will be determined by the different supply capabilities (transformation schedules) of the two countries. The **equilibrium terms of trade** will then be that terms-of-trade line at which one nation's desired quantity of auto imports will exactly match the other nation's desired quantity of auto exports in exchange for imported wheat.

For two nations of approximately equal size and similar demand patterns, one would expect the equilibrium terms of trade to be about halfway between the pre-trade domestic price ratios of the two nations. In this case the gains from trade would be distributed equally between the two nations. However, if one nation is considerably larger than the other, the equilibrium terms of trade would be quite close to the original domestic price ratio of that nation, in order that both nations desire equal amounts of exports and imports. In effect, the smaller nation in this case would benefit from a more favorable terms of trade and receive most of the gains from trade.

How does economic growth affect the gains from trade? Growth in productive capability is reflected in an outward shift in a nation's transformation schedule over time. If such growth applies primarily to the product in which the nation has a comparative advantage, it is said to be **export-biased growth**. Such a bias might arise from more agricultural equipment or improved agricultural technology in a wheat-exporting nation. By increasing the nation's willingness to export, this growth would have a tendency to worsen the nation's terms of trade, thereby reducing or offsetting some of the anticipated gains from growth. In extreme cases (often noted in theory but rarely identified in the real world), the terms of trade could deteriorate so much that even with economic growth the nation would end up on a lower indifference curve after trade than it had achieved before the economic growth took place; this case is given the name of **immiserizing growth**. Alternatively, if productivity growth applies primarily to a nation's ability to produce the item that it has been importing, the economic growth is said to be **import-biased**, and by reducing the nation's relative offer of exports this has a tendency to improve the nation's terms of trade. In effect, import-biased growth tends to reduce productive differences between nations, reducing the need for and the potential gains from trade.

As indicated above, the terms-of-trade ratio frequently is used to measure or estimate a nation's gains from international trade. The most frequently used indicator is the **commodity terms of trade**, or the ratio of a nation's export commodity price to its import commodity price. In the example used earlier, a flatter terms-of-trade line for a wheat-exporting nation would mean that it would give up fewer units of wheat for a given number of imported autos. Essentially, the price of wheat has risen relative to the price of autos, or the nation's commodity terms of trade has improved (in mathematical terms, the commodity terms of trade is the reciprocal or inverse of the slope of the terms-of-trade line). In the real world, where many products rather than only two are traded, a nation's commodity terms of trade is calculated as an index of that nation's export commodity prices relative to an index of its import prices. A rising commodity terms of trade generally signifies that a nation's gains from trade are increasing over time, although a more complete picture of a nation's import capacity requires a consideration not only of export and import prices but also of changes in volume or quantity of that nation's exports.

KEY CONCEPTS AND TERMS (Define each concept, and briefly explain its significance.)

Indifference curve

Community indifference curve

Marginal rate of substitution

Autarky (no-trade) equilibrium

Terms-of-trade line

Offer curve

Theory of reciprocal demand

Equilibrium production and consumption with trade

Equilibrium terms of trade

Export-biased growth

Immiserizing growth

Import-biased growth

Commodity terms of trade

TRUE OR FALSE? (On an exam, be prepared to explain *why* the statement is true or false.)

T F 1. An indifference curve shows the different combinations of goods (e.g., wheat and autos) that would provide equal value or satisfaction to an individual or a nation.

T F 2. For most individuals or nations, the marginal rate of substitution along an indifference curve is constant.

T F 3. International trade usually enables a nation to reach a higher community indifference curve than would be possible with autarky (no trade).

T F 4. With trade between two countries, the equilibrium terms of trade will equal the domestic price ratio that prevailed in the smaller country before trade began.

T F 5. Mill's theory of reciprocal demand shows that the equilibrium terms of trade between two nations depends only on production costs in the two nations.

T F 6. Between two nations of unequal size, most of the gains from trade are likely to go to the smaller nation.

T F 7. A labor-abundant country that grows over time primarily because of a larger labor supply is likely to experience import-biased growth.

T F 8. Export-biased growth is likely to worsen a nation's terms of trade.

T F 9. Immizerizing growth refers to a nation whose population is growing faster than its gross domestic production over time.

T F 10. A nation's commodity or barter terms of trade reflects its export prices relative to its import prices.

MULTIPLE CHOICE

1.	A community indifference curve is intended to show
	a.	what percentage of a country's people are indifferent to trade with other nations
	b.	how much of one product must be given up in order to produce one more unit of another product
	c.	combinations of consumer goods that would provide equal satisfaction for members of that community
	d.	in which product a country has a comparative advantage

2.	The marginal rate of substitution along an indifference curve
	a.	is constant for all combinations of wheat and autos
	b.	shows that after consumers accept less wheat for more autos, they will give up less wheat for even more autos
	c.	shows that after consumers accept less wheat for more autos, they will give up more wheat for even more autos
	d.	determines a country's comparative advantage

3.	Without trade, a nation achieves autarky equilibrium by
	a.	emphasizing production according to its comparative advantage
	b.	producing equal amounts of wheat and autos
	c.	employing half of its labor force in wheat production and the other half in auto production
	d.	producing and consuming at the point where the highest achievable community indifference curve is tangent to its transformation schedule

4.	When a nation specializes according to comparative advantage,
	a.	it shifts production toward more of its comparative advantage product and consumes on a higher indifference curve than would be attainable without trade
	b.	it shifts its transformation schedule outward
	c.	it shifts to a better point on its original community indifference curve
	d.	the price of its export product declines relative to the price of imports

5.	Mill's theory of reciprocal demand
	a.	proved Ricardo's theory of comparative advantage to be wrong
	b.	provided new support for Adam Smith's theory of absolute advantage
	c.	showed how both demand and supply must be considered to determine the equilibrium terms of trade between two nations
	d.	showed that demand rather than supply factors determine a nation's comparative advantage and terms of trade

6.	If trade occurs between a larger and a much smaller nation,
	a.	the larger nation will get most of the gains from trade
	b.	the smaller nation will get most of the gains from trade
	c.	the gains from trade will be shared equally
	d.	trade will benefit only the larger nation

7.	A country that exports labor-intensive goods and experiences a rapid growth in its labor force will have
	a.	import-biased growth
	b.	export-biased growth
	c.	neutral growth
	d.	a rapidly improving terms of trade

8. Immizerizing growth occurs for a nation
   a. if benefits from its expanding transformation schedule are more than negated by deteriorating terms of trade
   b. if its transformation schedule shifts inward when capital goods are not replaced as they wear out
   c. if its terms of trade improves faster than its labor force grows
   d. frequently throughout history, even though theory cannot yet explain this phenomenon

9. The commodity terms of trade
   a. is the opposite of a nation's barter terms of trade
   b. is the ratio of a nation's export price index to its import price index
   c. is the ratio of a nation's import price index to its export price index
   d. measures the cost of transporting commodities from one nation to another

10. The commodity terms of trade for oil-exporting countries
    a. rose from 1970 through 1990
    b. has been falling since the early 1960s
    c. fell during the 1960s, rose dramatically during the 1970s, and has declined again since the 1980s
    d. has remained relatively constant since 1945

PROBLEMS AND SHORT ANSWER QUESTIONS

1. Explain how the marginal rate of transformation differs from the marginal rate of substitution at point B on the graph below. Explain why the country will achieve a higher level of satisfaction at point A than at point B, and how this is reflected in the slopes of the transformation and indifference curves at point A.

20

2.   Explain how the changing terms of trade encourages the nation to move from point A to point B below, producing more autos and less wheat as it specializes through international trade. Explain also how it is able now to consume beyond its transformation curve, and why it would choose to be at point C rather than at point D or E. How does this represent the gains from international trade for this nation?

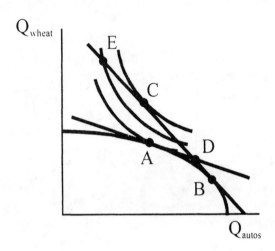

3.   Use a graph such as the one in Question 2 to explain how both supply and demand factors influence a nation's desire to trade, as reflected in Mill's theory of reciprocal demand. How would an increase or improvement in this nation's terms of trade affect its desire to export autos and import wheat?

4.   Explain the meaning of export-biased growth, and illustrate this on the graph below by shifting the nation's transformation schedule to reflect such growth. Under what circumstances might this even lead to immiserizing growth?

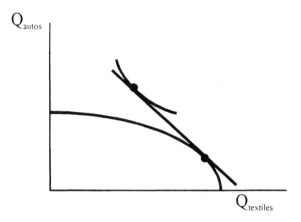

5.   Suppose that a nation's export price index was 102 in 1990 and 110 in 1992, and that its import price index was 90 in 1990 and 108 in 1992 (1985 = 100). Without making calculations, can you explain what happened to this nation's commodity terms of trade between 1985 and 1990? between 1985 and 1992? Calculate the terms of trade to show what happened to the commodity terms of trade between 1990 and 1992. Explain the significance of these trends.

EXPLORATIONS BEYOND THE CLASSROOM

1.   Locate newspaper or magazine articles dealing with recent growth experiences of specific developing countries, and search for evidence or indicators of whether such growth appears to have been either export-biased or import-biased in nature. For instance, examine the effects of the significant policy changes in Chile in recent years.

2.   Consult a recent issue of the IMF *International Financial Statistics* for examples of countries that have experienced improved terms of trade in recent years, and examples of other countries whose terms of trade have declined recently. Can you find any examples of countries that have experienced increased export earnings despite a declining export price index? Explain how this would be possible.

CHAPTER 4

TRADE MODEL EXTENSIONS AND APPLICATIONS

SYNOPSIS OF CHAPTER CONTENT

The theory of comparative advantage as presented by Ricardo identifies relative differences in labor productivity between nations as the source of comparative advantage but does not attempt to provide a theoretical explanation for such productivity differences. The primary objectives of this chapter are to explore and analyze various approaches to understanding more fully the sources of comparative advantage and to assess the ability of comparative advantage theory to explain actual trade patterns among nations.

Eli Heckscher and Bertil Ohlin formulated a theory in the 1920s and 1930s that identified different relative **factor endowments** as the source of comparative advantage among nations. For instance, if one country has a relative abundance of land and another country a relative abundance of capital, the first country will have a comparative advantage in producing and exporting a land-intensive product such as wheat, while the second country would have a comparative advantage in a capital-intensive product such as autos. Transformation schedules would be bowed out, because in each country some land and capital would be relatively better suited to wheat production and some to auto production. However, in the first country the transformation schedule would be extended farther out along the wheat axis because of land abundance, and in the second country it would be extended farther out along the auto axis because of capital abundance. If demand conditions (community indifference curves) are identical or at least similar in the two nations, price lines without trade will show wheat to be relatively inexpensive in the first country because of its land abundance, and autos to be relatively inexpensive in the second country because of its capital abundance. With trade, an equilibrium terms-of-trade line between the two initial extremes will induce the first country to shift toward more wheat production as wheat rose in price, while the second country will shift toward more auto production as autos rose in price in that country. Each nation will export the product that uses intensively the factor of production that is relatively abundant in that country, and import the product that uses intensively the factor of production which is scarce in that country. In effect, each nation gains access to scarce factors of production (land, capital, or labor) through trade, importing such resources **indirectly** through products intensive in their use.

A further implication of the **factor endowments theory** is that international trade tends to equalize not only the relative prices of products between nations (for instance, wheat and autos) but also the prices of factors of production. If we consider labor and capital to be the factors of production, pre-trade wage rates will be relatively low in the labor-abundant country and high in the labor-scarce country. With trade, the labor-abundant country will increase production of the labor-intensive product, and the labor-scarce country will shift away from such production. This production shift will strengthen the demand for labor and raise wage rates in the first country, and relieve such demand and reduce wage rates in the second country, thus bringing wage rates closer together. In similar fashion, capital costs or interest rates will converge as trade increases demand for capital in the capital-abundant country and as imports of capital-intensive products alleviate the scarcity of capital in the other country. Thus, international trade tends to bring about **factor-price equalization** between countries.

The conditions under which factor-price equalization occurs are quite restrictive, so we rarely find complete equalization of wage rates, interest rates, and rental rates among nations in the real world. However, the tendency toward such equalization does explain why increased trade among nations often brings with it a concern about the impact of such trade on the **distribution of income** within each nation. Within each nation, the returns to the scarce factor of production tend to fall, while the returns to the abundant factor tend to rise. Workers in capital-abundant countries resist the potential impact of trade on their wage rates, and owners of capital in labor-abundant countries fear that trade will bring lower interest rates in their country. The inclination to favor trade restrictions in each case is understandable, although the realization that each nation enjoys overall gains from trade according to comparative

23

advantage might encourage us rather to consider the use of internal government spending, taxation, and transfer programs to address the distributional impacts of trade.

How well does the Heckscher-Ohlin factor endowment theory explain actual trade patterns among nations? The most celebrated effort to test this theory was that of Wassily Leontief in 1954, who applied a mathematical input-output model of the U.S. economy to 1947 trade data. He found that the capital/labor ratio for U.S. export industries actually was lower than for U.S. import-competing industries, exactly the opposite of what the factor endowment theory would predict for a capital-abundant nation such as the United States. He later achieved similar results using 1951 trade data. Economists have developed a variety of theoretical and empirical explanations for what has come to be known as the **Leontief Paradox**. Most of these explanations essentially involve creating a more generalized factor endowment model, recognizing the importance of finer distinctions within the general categories of land, labor, and capital as factors of production. U.S. exports, for instance, were found to be intensive in their use of skilled labor, engineering talent, and research and development input; these are resources that the United States had in abundance relative to its trading partners.

One particular theory that reflects the importance of multiple factors of production is the **product life cycle theory**. According to this theory, new products developed through technological innovation are introduced first in a home market such as the United States, where both a large market and the resources important at this initial stage are found. During the second stage, the domestic industry develops a capacity for export, again reflecting comparative advantage within the context of a generalized factor endowment model. During the third stage, foreign production begins, usually in other industrial countries to which the home firms exported during the second stage. A fourth stage witnesses the loss of competitive advantage in the home market as the technological gap narrows, and during a final fifth stage the product becomes standardized and is imported into the original home market. Developing countries often gain a production advantage at this point, again in a manner consistent with the generalized factor endowment model since they have an abundance of the semi-skilled labor that becomes a more important input at this stage in the product life cycle.

One thing made more clear by these extensions of the Heckscher-Ohlin theory is that a nation's relative factor endowments easily may change over time. Industrial nations in Europe along with Japan have narrowed the technological gap that favored the United States after World War II. Several developing countries now are quite capable of operating near the middle or even toward the beginning of the product life cycle. Comparative advantage now must be viewed in dynamic terms, with a nation's ability to operate at the beginning of the product life cycle dependent on its continuing efforts to develop skilled labor, research scientists, and innovators with solid managerial and engineering talents. The term **industrial policy** has been introduced to recognize the potential role of government in helping to shape and develop a nation's **dynamic comparative advantage**.

Several other aspects of trade theory and trade patterns among nations deserve at least brief mention. Trade theory based on factor endowments generally assumes resources to be immobile among countries but perfectly mobile inside each country. However, if some resources such as capital are specific to individual industries, the distributional impacts of trade are altered. For instance, owners of specialized plants or equipment that are used in export industries will gain as trade opens up, while owners of specialized equipment that is limited to use in import-competing industries will lose from trade. These effects tend to be short-term rather than long-term in nature.

The presence of **economies of scale** in production also may influence trade patterns, generally encouraging nations to specialize to a greater extent in their comparative advantage industries than otherwise would be optimal; if economies of scale are extreme, they may specialize completely in production of export goods. The presence or expectation of economies of scale also can influence governments to support key industries in hopes of gaining advantage from experience and high-volume output.

A theory developed by Staffan Linder maintains that trade in manufactured goods occurs between countries with similar domestic demand conditions. Hypothesizing that similar tastes or preferences derive primarily from similar income levels, Linder predicted that trade in manufactured goods would occur between countries with **overlapping demands** as reflected in overlapping ranges of per capita income. Although detailed empirical support for this theory has not been found, it is evident that much trade in manufactures does occur among industrial nations, rather than between industrial and developing nations as the factor endowment theories would predict. Another important recent phenomenon that can be viewed within this general framework is the growing tendency toward **intraindustry trade**. Much of this trade within broad industry categories can be understood in terms of product differentiation, especially in oligopolistic industries where economies of scale are important; thus, many industrial nations export certain types of automobiles and import other types, for instance. The competition among industrial nations resulting from such intraindustry trade within the manufacturing sector also creates intense pressures for governments to adopt industrial policy strategies to protect and enhance domestic market and export market shares.

Another significant development in recent years is the expansion of trade in services, although we often tend to think of trade as involving primarily raw materials and manufactured products. Some services, such as transportation and tourism, traditionally have been a part of international trade. However, the growing importance of business services involving areas such as technology transfer, construction, engineering, consulting, accounting, banking, and finance has raised new questions about how the concept of comparative advantage might apply in these areas and about the often more subtle barriers that governments utilize to restrict the international flow of such services.

Finally, two other factors that influence international trade patterns but are not incorporated in simplified trade theories are transportation costs and environmental regulations. Transportation costs effectively prevent the complete international equalization of prices for traded goods, with the price in the importing nation exceeding that in the exporting nation by the amount of the transport costs. Some products either cannot be traded internationally or are prohibitively expensive to ship, but in other cases transportation costs simply reduce the volume of trade below what it would be without such costs. For some products, such as those involving natural resources, processing activities will be located either near the resources or near the final markets, depending on whether the processing is weight-losing or weight-gaining in nature.

In a similar manner, environmental regulations generally increase production costs. If such regulations deal with pollution effects from consumption, they increase product costs but do not directly affect production location. However, if the regulations deal with pollution which arises from production, such as that associated with steel production, they may affect production location and trade patterns by giving relative cost advantages to those nations with the least restrictive regulations. Some observers view such production shifts as legitimate or appropriate, while others call for international harmonization of environmental laws, offsetting subsidies, or countervailing trade barriers in order to prevent such shifts.

KEY CONCEPTS AND TERMS (Define each concept, and briefly explain its significance.)

Factor endowments

Heckscher-Ohlin factor endowments theory

25

Impact of trade on income distribution among factors of production

Factor-price equalization

Leontief paradox

Generalized factors of production model

Product life cycle theory

Dynamic comparative advantage

Industrial policy

Linder theory of overlapping demand

Interindustry versus intraindustry trade

Specific-factors trade model

Economies of scale

Transportation costs and trade

Environmental regulations and trade

TRUE OR FALSE? (On an exam, be prepared to explain *why* the statement is true or false.)

T F 1. In the factor endowment theory, a nation with more capital per worker than another nation will have a comparative advantage in capital-intensive products.

T F 2. The factor endowment theory predicts that trade will cause relative wages to fall in a labor-abundant nation.

T F 3. The Leontief paradox is that industrial nations tend to trade more with each other than with developing nations.

T F 4. The product life cycle model states that a new product will be produced throughout its lifetime in whatever nation first succeeds in introducing that product.

T F 5. Generalized factor endowment models emphasize the roles of different varieties of labor and capital in determining a nation's comparative advantage.

T F 6. The overlapping demand theory explains why trade often occurs between industrial nations with similar levels of per capita income.

T F 7. Owners of specialized equipment used only in a nation's export industry will tend to lose as that nation moves from self-sufficiency to more participation in trade.

T F 8. Dynamic comparative advantage recognizes that a nation's export patterns will shift as products move through the life cycle and relative factor endowments change.

T F 9. The existence of transportation costs often causes a reversal of comparative advantage between nations.

T F10. Strict U.S. laws on auto exhaust emissions create a production advantage for Japanese auto firms over domestic firms in the United States.

MULTIPLE CHOICE

1. In the Heckscher-Ohlin factor endowment theory of comparative advantage,
    a. the transformation schedule is a straight line, as in the Ricardian theory
    b. labor is the only relevant factor of production
    c. a nation's comparative advantage depends on how well endowed it is with specific factors of production such as labor and capital, relative to its trading partners
    d. the nation with the largest labor force will have a comparative advantage in labor-intensive products

2. In the Heckscher-Ohlin theory, two nations have the potential for mutual gains from trade with each other if
   a. they have similar levels of per capita income
   b. their transformation schedules reflect different relative abilities to produce labor- and capital-intensive goods, based on their relative resource endowments
   c. the tastes or preferences of people in one country differ significantly from those of people in the other country
   d. transportation costs are zero

3. If a labor-abundant nation trades freely with a capital-abundant nation, there will be a tendency for
   a. wages to rise relative to capital costs in both nations
   b. wages to fall relative to capital costs in both nations
   c. wages to rise in the first nation relative to wages in the second nation
   d. wages to fall in the first nation relative to wages in the second nation

4. The empirical finding known as the Leontief paradox was that
   a. U.S. exports were more labor-intensive than U.S. imports, even though the United States is regarded as a capital-abundant nation
   b. the United States traded more with other industrial nations than with developing nations
   c. trade reduced rather than increased the welfare of citizens in the United States
   d. U.S. exports grew much less rapidly than U.S. GNP over time

5. Potential explanations for the Leontief paradox include all of the following *except*:
   a. the United States imposed high tariffs on labor-intensive imports
   b. the United States actually has a larger relative labor force than its major trading partners
   c. U.S. exports are intensive in their use of skilled labor
   d. the United States tends to export high-technology products that require significant scientific and engineering inputs

6. According to the product life cycle model,
   a. the nation that begins producing and exporting a new product will continue to do so until the product becomes obsolete
   b. products initially imported into the United States will later be produced in the United States, once the market becomes established
   c. the United States has a comparative advantage in products with short life cycles
   d. a new product initially produced in the United States may later be exported from developing nations to the United States, once it becomes a mature, standardized product

7. Linder's overlapping demand theory of trade
   a. helps to explain the extensive trade between industrial and developing nations
   b. maintains that manufactured goods are first produced for the home market, then exported to nations with similar levels of per capita GNP
   c. strongly supports the factor endowment theory of comparative advantage
   d. explains why nations specialize completely, and do not produce at home any of the products they import

8. The growing importance of intraindustry trade
   a. reflects the declining importance of economies of scale
   b. explains why governments are reluctant to adopt aggressive industrial policies
   c. primarily involves homogeneous products
   d. often involves differentiated products in industries where economies of scale are present

9. Differences in environmental regulations between nations are most likely to affect production location and trade patterns when
   a. the regulations deal with consumption pollution such as food safety or auto exhaust emissions
   b. the regulations deal with production pollution such as air pollution from steel manufacturing
   c. regulations deal with either consumption or production pollution; the type is not important
   d. international subsidies are used to equalize the standards

10. The existence of transportation costs in international trade
    a. creates a gap between the prices of goods in the exporting nation and in the importing nation, and reduces the volume of trade
    b. often reverses or changes the pattern of trade predicted by the factor endowment model
    c. means that processing activities will be located near the source of raw materials if the processing is weight-gaining in nature
    d. means that complete factor-price equalization between nations is more likely to occur

PROBLEMS AND SHORT ANSWER QUESTIONS

1. Assume that Mexico has a higher labor-to-capital ratio than the United States, leaving the United States well endowed with capital relative to Mexico. Assume also that clothing is labor-intensive in production relative to autos.

   a. Use the factor endowment theory framework to label the two transformation schedules below, indicating which one represents Mexico and which one represents the United States.

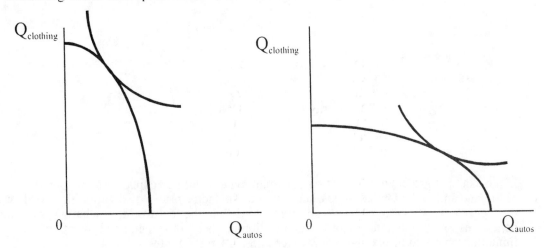

b. Assuming similar tastes or preferences as reflected in the two indifference curves shown in part a, draw the pre-trade price line for each country. Which one is steeper? What does this mean? In which country are autos relatively more expensive? Does this make sense, given what you know about production capabilities in each nation?

c. Now draw a pair of international terms-of-trade lines (one on each diagram) to illustrate the potential for trade between Mexico and the United States. Why must these lines be parallel to each other? Why will the new price line for the United States be steeper than the pre-trade line? Why will the new line for Mexico be flatter than before trade? Explain in words what this means. Show and explain how production will shift in each country according to comparative advantage. Draw an additional indifference curve for each country to show the new consumption point. Identify the desired amounts of exports and imports for each country. What must be true if the terms-of-trade lines that you drew generate equilibrium in trade between Mexico and the United States? If you find that the United States would offer to export more autos than Mexico would like to import at the selected price ratio, would your terms-of-trade line need to become steeper or flatter to bring about equilibrium? Explain why, and what this means in terms of auto and clothing prices.

2.   In the example presented in Question 1, explain what would be expected to happen to wage rates in Mexico and in the United States, according to the factor-price equalization theory. How does this help to explain labor concerns about free trade? In the real world, in what ways are the conditions for complete factor-price equalization unlikely to be met, and how might these limitations apply to the example of Mexico and the United States?

3.	How do the various explanations for the Leontief paradox, and frameworks such as the product life cycle theory, help to create a more "dynamic" comparative advantage theory and illustrate how nations may either gain or lose specific comparative advantages as they enhance or neglect their productive resources over time?

4.	How do the existence of economies of scale and the Linder theory of overlapping demands help to explain the phenomenon of intraindustry trade? Why does this relate more to trade among industrial nations than to trade between industrial and developing nations? Which of these trade patterns do the traditional approaches to comparative advantage more effectively explain?

5.	It is easy to visualize trade in products. Try to explain, with specific examples, how trade can take place in services. Why is the volume of trade in business services growing, and how can we go about trying to explain a nation's comparative advantage in exporting certain types of business services?

6.   How do environmental regulations established by national governments affect international trade patterns? Why is it important to distinguish between consumption pollution and production pollution in analyzing this impact? For instance, why would strict air pollution standards for steel production be expected to have an impact on trade and foreign investment patterns, whereas stiff U.S. environmental standards on auto exhaust emissions would not?

EXPLORATIONS BEYOND THE CLASSROOM

1.   Find examples in recent newspapers or magazines of U.S. industries that appear to be in the first stages of the product life cycle and to show good export potential. Locate other examples dealing with domestic industries that are facing serious competition from imports. Do these appear in any way to represent industries in the later stages of the product life cycle?

2.   Consult recent statistical sources on the composition of U.S. exports and imports to find examples of intraindustry trade. Do you also find examples of exports or imports that are more easily explainable in traditional comparative advantage terms?

3.   Locate articles dealing with the opposition of U.S. labor organizations or other interest groups to free trade, and see if the concerns of these groups can be understood in terms of the redistribution predictions of the factor-price equalization theory.

4.   Consult magazines dealing with environmental issues for examples of conflicts within the United States between protecting the environment and keeping industry and jobs at home. Look also for examples of developing countries reluctant to strengthen environmental policies in order to attract foreign investment from industrial nations.

5.   Review news coverage of the protests during the November 1999 World Trade Organization (WTO) meetings in Seattle, Washington, and during WTO meetings held since that time. How do these protests reflect the concerns of U.S. labor and environmental groups about the effects of free trade on jobs and the environment? How have economists and other commentators responded to these protest arguments?

CHAPTER 5

TARIFFS

SYNOPSIS OF CHAPTER CONTENT

The central message of our review of international trade and trade theory to this point has been that nations can achieve mutual benefits from trading with each other. The implication of this analysis, and of comparative advantage theory, is that a policy of free trade would be superior to policies that restrict international trade among nations. Yet we find that most nations, both today and throughout history, have used a variety of barriers to limit trade rather than pursuing free trade policies. The objective of this chapter is to consider the impacts of the tariff, one of the most common barriers to international trade.

Simply put, a tariff is a tax on international trade. The most common such tax is an **import tariff**, although some nations also levy taxes or duties on exports in the form of an **export tariff**. As with a domestic tax, a tariff on imports both generates money for the government and affects the level of activity being taxed. Thus, an import tariff will have a **revenue effect** in the form of taxes collected and also a **protective effect** in that it discourages imports and also promotes domestic production for the local market sheltered by the tariff.

A tariff generally takes the form of a **specific tariff**, a fixed amount of money per physical unit of imports (for instance, 16.5 cents per kilogram of mercury), or an **ad valorem tariff**, a percentage of the value of imported items (for instance, a 4 percent tariff on imported auto tires). In some cases these are combined in a **compound tariff**, requiring an importer to pay a fixed amount of duty plus a percentage of the value of imported products. Determining the amount of an ad valorem tariff requires a valuation measure of the imported product; the United States traditionally has used the **free-on-board** (FOB) method, reflecting the product value as it leaves the exporting nation, while a number of other nations use the more comprehensive **cost-insurance-freight** (CIF) method, including transportation costs and thus reflecting the product value as it reaches the importing nation.

The effects of a 10 percent ad valorem tariff are shown on the following graph. The 10 percent tariff will raise the domestic price above the world price by 10 percent, assuming that the importing nation is too small to influence the world price by its trade policies. Domestic production rises from Q_1 to Q_2 as local firms respond to the higher price with increased output. Imports fall from Q_1Q_4 to Q_2Q_3 as foreign firms receive a smaller share of a declining market (total demand falls, and domestic production rises, as the price goes up).

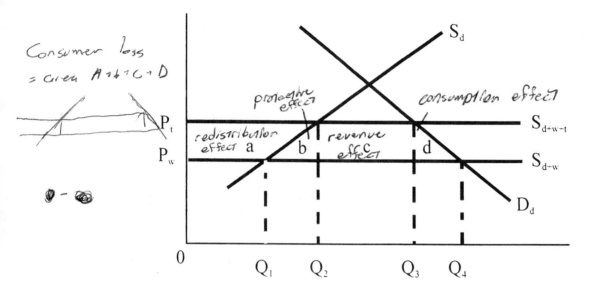

Consumer loss
= area A + b + C + D

This tariff will have several different effects:

Consumers will lose benefits in the form of **consumer surplus** (consumption benefits above and beyond what they pay to purchase the product) equal to the sum of areas *a, b, c,* and *d* on the graph, as they buy less at a higher price.

Domestic firms receive a portion of this loss in the form of a **redistribution effect**, equal to area *a,* as their increased revenues exceed their increased costs from expanding production (an increase in profits).

Domestic firms also receive an amount equal to area *b* known as the **protective effect**, which compensates them for their higher cost of production (their inefficiency relative to foreign firms) as they expand production from Q_1 to Q_2.

The domestic government benefits from the **revenue effect** equal to area *c,* representing the tariff revenue collected on the imported products.

The remaining part of the consumer surplus loss, area *d,* is the **consumption effect**, reflecting the net loss to consumers from reducing their purchases in response to the higher price caused by the tariff.

The net impact is that the nation imposing the tariff suffers a welfare loss equal to the sum of areas *b* and *d,* representing the extent to which the loss to consumers exceeds the gain to domestic producers in the form of profits and the gain to the government in the form of tariff revenue. Stated differently, by imposing a tariff the nation loses some of the gains it would have derived from free trade with other nations. The effects of a specific tariff would be identical to those shown for this ad valorem tariff, except that the price would rise by the dollar amount of the tariff rather than as a percentage of the initial

34

world price of the product. Over time, of course, the dollar amount of an ad valorem tariff will vary as the price of the product changes, whereas a specific tariff would remain fixed in amount unless changed by the government.

This analysis relates to the "small-nation case," in which the nation imposing the tariff is so small that its willingness to import has no impact on the world price of the product. A nation that constitutes a significant share of the world market for the product, however, may induce exporting nations to lower their prices in response to the tariff, as shown in the "large-nation case." As shown in the following graph, such a nation faces an upward-sloping rather than a horizontal world supply curve for imports. A specific tariff of 10 dollars raises the foreign or world supply curve by 10 dollars, but as indicated the domestic price rises by less than the full 10-dollar amount, and the net price received by the exporting nation falls by the remainder of the 10 dollars. For instance, if the price rises by 8 dollars the exporter will receive 2 dollars less than before the tariff was imposed. The revenue effect of the tariff in this case is area c plus area e, but area e represents the loss to foreign producers as they now provide imports Q_2Q_3 at a lower price than before. In this case, the nation may actually gain from the tariff if this transfer from foreign producers (area e) exceeds the net loss identified earlier (areas b and d).

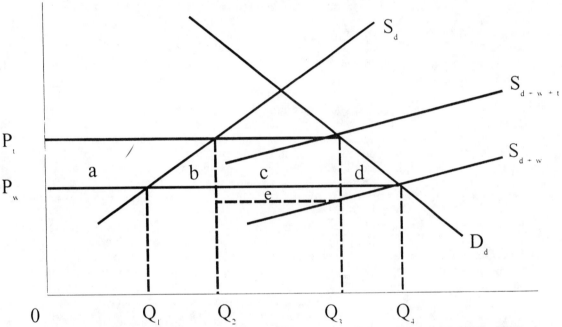

It should be noted that the outside nations suffer welfare losses when a nation imposes a tariff, in the form of reduced sales in the small-nation case and also in lower export prices in the large-nation case. Thus, global welfare almost certainly is reduced by the tariff, an impact that will be compounded if trading partners respond to tariffs with retaliation, imposing trade barriers of their own.

Thus far the analysis has focused on the **nominal tariff rate** (the published tariff), which does not always provide an adequate indicator of how much protection tariffs confer on economic activity within a nation. The concept of **effective protection** is designed to do this. The **effective tariff rate** takes into account not only the tariff on the product itself, but also the tariffs on inputs for that product in determining the amount of protection received by a particular activity. Thus, the effective tariff rate measures the percentage by which an industry can increase its cost of production or value added as a result of the entire structure of nominal tariffs on its output and its inputs. For example, consider a shoe manufacturer that purchases materials for $24 and transforms them into shoes that sell for $40. A 10 percent ad valorem tariff on shoes would enable this domestic producer to raise the price to $44. But if there were no tariffs on imported materials such as leather, the value added by this producer would increase from $16 ($40 - $24) to $20 ($44 - $24); this gives the domestic firm an effective protective margin of 25 percent compared with a foreign shoe manufacturer, rather than simply 10 percent as the nominal tariff rate suggests.

In general, the effective tariff rate is determined as follows:

if n = the nominal tariff rate on the final product,
          a = the ratio of the value of the inputs to the value of the final product,
     $1 - a$ = the value added by the producer or activity under consideration, and
          b = the nominal tariff rate on imported inputs,

then the effective tariff rate is

$$e = (n - ab)/(1 - a).$$

Using values from the earlier example, we find that materials represent 60 percent of the value of manufactured shoes, with value added representing the other 40 percent, so with a nominal tariff on imported shoes of 10 percent and no tariff on inputs, the effective rate of protection is

$$e = [0.1 - 0.6(0)]/(1 - 0.6) = 0.1/0.4 = 0.25,$$

showing that the activity of manufacturing shoes receives an effective protective margin of 25 percent, rather than simply the 10 percent implied by the nominal tariff rate on imported shoes.

Two aspects of this concept and equation deserve emphasis. First, the nominal tariff understates the effective tariff rate to a greater extent for an activity that adds relatively little to the value of the materials it transforms (for instance, automobile assembly) than for an activity for which the value added is a larger share of the final product; in other words, a high value of a increases the value of e. Second, an increase in tariffs on imported inputs will lower the effective protection for the industry or activity using those inputs; a high value of b reduces the value of e. Thus, a higher tariff on imported steel would reduce the effective protection for the auto industry or any other industries that use steel as an input.

The concept of effective protection becomes important in analyzing the impact of an **escalated tariff structure**, which is a common feature in industrial nations. Such nations often impose no tariffs or very low tariffs on imported raw materials, moderate tariffs on imported intermediate products, and even higher tariffs on finished products. This means that for any economic activity, the nominal tariffs on inputs are lower than the nominal tariff on what is produced at that stage, creating an effective rate of protection that is higher than the nominal tariff rate. Among other things, this escalated tariff structure and the resulting high rates of effective protection for value-adding activities make it difficult for raw-materials exporters in developing countries to establish processing and manufacturing operations for exporting finished products to industrial nations. Finally, it should be noted that the effective tariff rate is simply equivalent to the nominal tariff rate for a nation that sets identical nominal tariffs on all imports and thus does not have an escalated tariff structure.

What does this analysis imply for trade policy? We have seen that the welfare losses to consumers within nations that impose tariffs usually exceed the gains to domestic producers (higher profits) and to the domestic government (tariff revenue). This reinforces our earlier conclusion that nations gain from free-trade policies that encourage them to specialize according to comparative advantage and to import those products that other nations can produce more efficiently. Yet most nations do impose tariffs and other trade barriers.

One frequently offered justification for trade barriers is the protection of domestic jobs. An overlooked consequence of tariffs intended to protect jobs is that trade is a two-way street, and that reduced imports for one nation eventually are likely to bring job losses in the export sector, as other nations respond to their reduced exports and income by importing less from the tariff-imposing nation. Still, jobs protected

36

by import restrictions are more immediate and visible than those at risk in the export sector, so political pressures tend to favor trade restrictions.

Another argument for trade restrictions is the need to protect domestic workers from cheap foreign labor. This is a variant of the job-protection argument. It fails to recognize that foreign competitiveness depends not only on wage rates but also on labor productivity; in cases where productivity does give low-wage nations a cost advantage, all nations would benefit by allowing such nations to produce and export according to their comparative advantages. An extreme form of the cheap foreign labor argument seeks to justify the **scientific tariff**, whereby a nation sets tariffs individually on each product so as to offset or neutralize any cost advantages such as those resulting from lower labor costs. The logical extension of this argument would be to set prohibitive tariffs, eliminating all trade and foregoing the potential gains from specialization according to comparative advantage.

Finally, support for tariffs and other trade barriers frequently comes from those wishing to promote **fair trade** or to create a **level playing field** for trading partners. Another often persuasive rationale is a dynamic trade policy argument to support **infant industries** with temporary tariff protection until they are able to become efficient producers and withstand global competition in a free trading environment. These and other arguments against free-trade policies will be considered more fully in later discussions of commercial and industrial policy.

KEY CONCEPTS AND TERMS (Define each concept, and briefly explain its significance.)

Specific tariff

Ad valorem tariff

Compound tariff

Nominal tariff rate

Producer and consumer surplus

Consumer surplus loss from tariff

Redistributive effect of tariff

37

Protective effect of tariff

Revenue effect of tariff

Deadweight consumer loss from tariff

Small-nation model of tariff effects

Large-nation model and terms-of-trade effects of tariff

Effective tariff rate

Escalated tariff structure

Protectionism

Beggar-thy-neighbor policy

Scientific tariff argument for protection

38

Infant-industry argument for protection

TRUE OR FALSE? (On an exam, be prepared to explain *why* the statement is true or false.)

T F 1.   A 10 percent tariff on imported shoes is an example of an ad valorem tariff.

T F 2.   A 10 percent tariff based on an FOB customs valuation has a larger dollar magnitude than a 10 percent tariff based on a CIF customs valuation.

T F 3.   The protective effect of a tariff refers to the increased profits earned by domestic producers of the product.

T F 4.   A tariff that is high enough to exclude all imports also will have a significant revenue effect.

T F 5.   If a small nation imposes a tariff on imports, the loss to its consumers will be smaller than the gains from domestic profits and government tariff revenue.

T F 6.   A large nation may gain from imposing a tariff if the tariff leads foreign producers to reduce significantly their export prices.

T F 7.   Nominal tariff rates understate the effective tariff rates in nations that have escalated tariff structures.

T F 8.   The use of scientific tariffs is designed to support and reinforce a nation's comparative advantage.

T F 9.   The infant-industry argument supports temporary tariffs as a new industry achieves efficiency through experience.

T F10.   The "level playing field" approach to trade policy often includes the use of tariffs in response to perceived unfair import barriers established by trading partners.

MULTIPLE CHOICE

1.   A nominal $1 tariff per pair of imported shoes is
    a.   an export tariff
    b.   an ad valorem tariff
    c.   a specific tariff
    d.   an effective tariff rate

2.   The benefit that a tariff provides for domestic firms to compensate for their inefficiency relative to foreign producers is the
    a.   redistributive effect
    b.   protective effect
    c.   revenue effect
    d.   consumption effect, or deadweight consumer loss

3.   The increased profits that a tariff provides for domestic firms is the
     a.   redistributive effect
     b.   protective effect
     c.   revenue effect
     d.   consumption effect, or deadweight consumer loss

4.   Foreign trade zones
     a.   are approved shipping lanes for ocean transport
     b.   create barriers to imports, but without establishing formal tariffs
     c.   enable foreign producers to avoid the payment of import tariffs
     d.   enable domestic companies to defer duties on imported inputs until they are processed
          and shipped to market

5.   A tariff quota
     a.   establishes a lower tariff on an initial quantity of imports, and a higher tariff on imports
          beyond that level
     b.   is a quantitative limit on the number of tariffs that a country can impose on imports
     c.   raises domestic prices by less than a simple tariff would
     d.   generates no revenue for the national government

6.   If a small nation imposes a tariff (small-nation model),
     a.   the price rises by less than the amount of the tariff
     b.   the losses to domestic consumers exceed the gains to domestic firms and to the domestic
          government
     c.   foreign producers will stop exporting to this nation rather than paying the tariff
     d.   there will be no revenue effect

7.   If a large nation imposes a tariff (large-nation model),
     a.   the price rises by more than the amount of the tariff
     b.   the price rises by exactly the amount of the tariff
     c.   the nation will stop importing because domestic firms will supply the entire market
     d.   the net loss to consumers may be less than the benefits from improved terms of trade

8.   The effective tariff rate or effective rate of protection is
     a.   always equal to the nominal ad valorem tariff rate
     b.   lower than the nominal tariff rate if nominal tariffs on inputs are lower than the tariff on
          imports of an industry's final product
     c.   higher than the nominal tariff rate if nominal tariffs on inputs are lower than the tariff on
          imports of an industry's final product
     d.   equal to the nominal tariff rate on imports of an industry's product only if tariffs on
          inputs are zero

9.   The argument that saving jobs at home requires tariffs to offset the advantages of lower wages in
     other countries
     a.   is called the infant-industry argument for protection
     b.   is valid whenever unemployment exists within the country, although not if there is full
          employment
     c.   is a strategic way for a nation to improve its comparative advantage
     d.   does not consider the impact of labor productivity differences or the potential for
          comparative disadvantage

10.   "Fair" trade policies to create a "level playing field"
    a.   are supported more by export industries than by import-competing industries
    b.   are designed to establish import barriers that are comparable to those imposed by a
            nation's trading partners
    c.   ensure that all nations move toward free-trade policies
    d.   help a nation to recapture the gains from trade that it lost when other nations placed
            tariffs on its imports

PROBLEMS AND SHORT ANSWER QUESTIONS

1.   Use the following graph to answer the questions below.

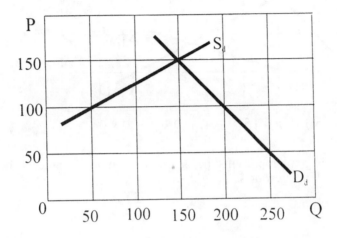

    a.   What would be the price of steel in the United States if a policy of "self-sufficiency"
            were established and no imports were allowed? How many tons of steel would be
            produced?

    b.   If the world price of steel were $100 per ton and the United States adopted a free-trade
            policy, identify on the graph and state below how much steel would be produced in the
            United States, and how much would be imported.

    c.   Show on the graph and determine the dollar magnitudes of the different effects of a 20
            percent tariff on steel imports.

                        Total consumer surplus loss   _____
                        Redistributive effect   _____
                        Protective effect   _____
                        Revenue effect   _____
                        Consumption effect   _____

41

d.   Briefly explain whether the United States as a nation would gain or lose in net terms
       from this tariff, and indicate the magnitude of this net gain or loss.

2.   Use the following graph to answer the questions below.

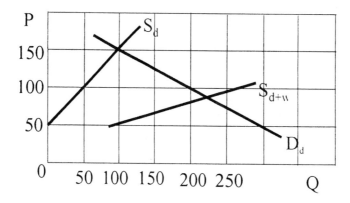

a.   Explain how this graph represents the "large-nation model," rather than the "small-nation
       model" reflected in Question 1.

b.   Identify on the graph and state the price, the quantity of domestic production, and the
       quantity of imports that would result from a free-trade policy.

c.   Suppose now that the United States imposes a specific duty of $20 per ton on imported
       steel. Show on the graph how this will affect price, domestic production, and imports of
       steel. Explain why the price will not rise by the full amount of the tariff.

d.   Show on the graph and determine the dollar magnitudes of the following effects of this tariff:

Total consumer surplus loss   _____
Redistributive effect   _____
Protective effect   _____
Domestic revenue effect   _____
Terms-of-trade effect   _____
Consumption effect   _____

e.   Explain the conditions under which a country might gain from a tariff, and determine whether it would do so in this case.

3.   Suppose that the United States imposes a 10 percent ad valorem tariff on imported clothing, but no tariffs on imports of fabrics or other inputs to the manufacture of clothing. Suppose also that the cost of such materials would be $32 for a $40 item of finished clothing, with the remaining $8 representing value added by the clothing manufacturer.

a.   What percentage of the final product does value-added represent in this example? Calculate the effective rate of protection for clothing manufacturing. Explain what this means, and why it is greater than 10 percent.

b.   Now suppose that a tariff of 5 percent also is imposed on imported inputs into clothing manufacturing. What is the new effective rate of protection for clothing manufacturing? Explain why this rate has declined but still exceeds 10 percent. How does this reflect the phenomenon of an escalated tariff structure?

c.   Finally, suppose that the tariff on clothing inputs is raised to 10 percent, so the nominal tariffs on clothing and on inputs to clothing all are equal to 10 percent. Calculate the effective rate of protection for clothing manufacturing. What does this tell you about the relationship between nominal and effective tariff rates when all nominal rates are equal to each other and tariff structures are not escalated?

4.   Explain the meaning of an escalated tariff structure, and discuss how the escalated tariffs of industrial nations affect the ability of developing nations to process their raw materials for export rather than remaining exporters of primary commodities with lower value added.

5.   In recent years Chile has been reducing its tariffs, to the point where today a nominal 10 per cent tariff applies to virtually all import products. Chile plans to reduce this to a flat 6 per cent rate by the year 2003. Explain how this transition to a flat and now lower nominal tariff structure changes the effective protection received by different manufacturing industries in Chile.

6.   "Tariffs on imports from Mexico are necessary to protect jobs and wages of workers in the United States, and will only have minor negative effects on other groups within the United States." Carefully evaluate the logic of this statement, with reference to the different identifiable effects of a tariff.

7.   What is the infant-industry argument for tariff protection? Briefly discuss the strengths and limitations of this rationale for tariffs. If new industries require support, what methods other than import tariffs might be used?

8.   What are the arguments in favor of pursuing a "fair" trade policy, designed to achieve a "level playing field"? If most nations adopted such policies, how might this lead to higher rather than lower levels of tariff protection over time?

EXPLORATIONS BEYOND THE CLASSROOM

1.   Consult recent issues of the U.S. International Trade Commission's *Tariff Schedules of the United States* for examples of the types and levels of import tariffs established by the United States, and for examples of significant changes in these levels over time.

2.   Consult recent General Agreement on Tariffs and Trade publications to compare among nations tariff rates established on individual products. What differences do you observe, either among industrial nations or between industrial and developing nations? Do you find evidence of escalated tariff structures for industrial nations such as the European Community members, Japan, or the United States?

3.   Review recent newspapers or magazines for articles on trade policy controversies such as whether NAFTA should be extended to include other Latin American nations, or whether the United States should provide more protection for a specific industry. Try to summarize the key aspects of the controversy, to identify which of the most common arguments for protection are reflected in the articles, and to evaluate the validity of the arguments presented.

CHAPTER 6

NONTARIFF TRADE BARRIERS

SYNOPSIS OF CHAPTER CONTENT

Although tariffs may represent the most well-known form of trade restrictions, in recent decades various types of **nontariff trade barriers** (NTBs) have grown in significance, both because nations have relied more on such devices and because their relative importance has increased as nations have reduced the levels of their tariff protection through international negotiations.

One of the most common forms of nontariff trade barriers is the **import quota**. Whereas a tariff imposes a tax on imports, a quota imposes a quantitative limit on the volume of imports permitted over a specified period of time, generally a year. An import quota may be **global**, with no further imports permitted from any nation once the quantitative limit is reached, or **selective**, with specific portions of the global quota allocated to selected individual exporting nations.

The welfare effects of a quota are similar in many respects to those of a tariff. As shown in the first figure in Chapter 5, in the small nation case a tariff will raise the domestic price of the imported product by the amount of the tariff, from P_w to P_t, and the volume of imports will decline from Q_1Q_4 to Q_2Q_3. Imposing a quota on imports that is equivalent in magnitude to the level of imports resulting from a tariff will raise the domestic price by the same amount that such a tariff would. Only at this price will the gap between domestic demand and domestic production be just equal to the permitted quantity of imports; any price below this level would leave excess demand, creating upward pressure on the price. Because of this equivalent price increase, the redistributive, protective, and consumption effects of the quota are identical to those of the tariff.

However, the revenue effect of a tariff is different with a quota, since the quota does not impose a tax on imports. An equivalent amount of revenue might be captured by the domestic government if it auctions quota rights to the highest bidders among foreign export firms, or it might go to domestic import firms if they can bargain favorably with foreign export firms; in most cases, however, this revenue is captured by the foreign exporting firms as they sell their exports at the now higher price without being required to pay any tariff. Thus, the net welfare loss to a nation imposing a quota includes not only the protective effect and the consumption effect as with a tariff, but most likely also an amount equal to the revenue effect.

In addition to these short-term or static differences between tariffs and quotas, there also is an important long-term or dynamic difference. Over a period of time, demand for imported products is likely to grow as the importing nation's income increases. With a tariff in place, this outward shift of the demand curve would simply lead to an increase in imports, and the world price plus the tariff would constitute a ceiling above which the domestic price could not rise. However, with a quota in place it is not possible for imports to expand in response to the demand increase. The entire increase in demand will need to be met by increased domestic production, requiring a domestic price increase large enough for the movement along the upward-sloping domestic supply curve to bring forth the necessary output expansion. These price increases can be averted only if the government increases the amount of the quota enough to meet the growing demand. Thus, a quota not only creates greater immediate welfare losses to the imposing nation than would an equivalent tariff, it also brings inflation over time as domestic demand for the imported product expands, which would not occur under a tariff.

Nations occasionally impose a trade barrier that combines features of both tariffs and quotas, known as a **two-tier tariff** or a **tariff-rate quota**. A low nominal tariff rate is established for an initial limited quantity of imports, and a higher tariff for any imports in excess of the initial "quota." One stated reason for this approach is to minimize the negative impact on consumers by setting a lower tariff for within-quota imports, but in fact the extent of the price increase is determined by the tariff rate for above-quota imports. The nation actually loses welfare in comparison with using a single tariff, by transferring as windfall profits some of the tariff revenue to those foreign producers who supply the within-quota exports.

Another form of nontariff trade barrier that has become more prevalent in recent decades is the **orderly marketing agreement**, which is essentially a market-sharing pact negotiated between an importing nation and its trading partners. Orderly marketing agreements most often take the form of voluntary quotas known as **voluntary export restraints** (VERs). Such restraints may appear to be less protectionist than tariffs or formal quotas, but because they often are accepted only in order to avoid the imposition of mandatory import barriers their "voluntary" nature is subject to question. The welfare effects of VERs are similar to those of quotas, except that their voluntary nature prevents the government of the importing nation from capturing any of the revenue effect of a tariff by auctioning quota rights. Because the participants in VERs often include only the most important exporting nations, they sometimes create opportunities for other (usually higher-cost) suppliers to capture some of the market as prices rise in the importing nation. This secondary effect reduces the welfare loss to domestic consumers by moderating the price increase caused by the VER, but it also constitutes **trade diversion**, reducing global production efficiency by shifting some of the import market from the most efficient exporting nations to nonrestrained suppliers in other nations.

Most of our discussion of trade and trade policy has implicitly assumed that domestic goods are produced entirely at home, while imported items are produced entirely in foreign nations. The reality is that in today's global economy many manufactured goods that are finished or assembled at home include parts or components produced in other nations, a process known as foreign sourcing. A type of nontariff trade barrier developed to encourage use of domestic components is the **domestic content requirement**. Such local or domestic content requirements specify the minimum percentage of a product's value that must be produced within the country in order to be considered a domestic product not subject to tariffs or quotas. Some developing nations have used local content requirements to implement industrialization strategies based on import substitution (substituting domestic production for previous imports of manufactured goods). In recent years, labor unions in the United States have pressed for the introduction of such requirements to protect jobs in the U.S. auto industry. These requirements would limit the foreign sourcing of U.S. auto manufactures, but would apply with equal force to the U.S. production facilities of foreign auto manufacturers. Local content requirements have the effect of increasing production costs and prices by requiring firms to locate certain production facilities in the higher-cost importing nation. The welfare effects are similar to those of a quota, except that part of what would have been the revenue effect of an equivalent tariff goes to foreign producers as a deadweight loss to compensate for the higher-cost production inefficiencies rather than simply in the form of higher profits.

Rather than using tariffs or nontariff trade barriers to protect domestic producers, governments sometimes use **domestic subsidies** to achieve the same objective. A per-unit subsidy to domestic producers effectively shifts their supply curve down by the amount of the subsidy, with a **producer surplus** or **redistributive effect** in the form of increased profits for the more efficient domestic firms and a **protective effect** to compensate for the higher production costs of the less efficient firms. By not distorting the decisions of consumers, as would the higher prices caused by tariffs or quotas, subsidies protect domestic firms with lower welfare losses than those associated with tariffs or quotas. However, domestic subsidies must be financed by taxes, and the net impact on the nation using such subsidies depends on whether this tax burden is offset eventually by a strengthened domestic industry.

Governments also may attempt to influence trade patterns by promoting exports through the use of **export subsidies**. Such subsidies function as a negative tax on exports, shifting the export supply curve down by the amount of the per-unit subsidy. This has both a **terms-of-trade** effect, reducing the price of the nation's export product, and an **export revenue effect**, increasing the nation's export revenue as long as foreign demand is elastic (with export volume increasing by more than the price falls in percentage terms). Although the export subsidy will increase export volume, citizens of the subsidizing nation may lose as export prices fall relative to import prices and as they pay the taxes required to finance the export subsidies. A variant of the export subsidy is the **export credit subsidy**, whereby the government of the exporting nation provides or guarantees credit to foreign purchasers of expensive durables such as domestically produced aircraft. Again, such subsidies provide clear benefits to the foreign purchaser, but the net impact on the exporting nation is more difficult to assess.

Another form of trade barrier arises in response to **dumping**, which generally is defined as selling exports at prices below the cost of production, and from a practical standpoint is identified as selling a product in foreign markets at prices that are lower than the price charged in the domestic market. The motivation for such dumping may be (1) **sporadic**, in order to sell excess inventories during periods of slack demand or recession at home, (2) **predatory**, designed to undercut and eliminate foreign competition and gain monopoly control of a concentrated industry, or (3) **persistent**, whereby a producer with monopoly power engages in international price discrimination to increase global profits by charging higher prices in markets with relatively inelastic demand.

Although dumping confers benefits on domestic consumers in the form of lower-priced imports, governments in importing nations often respond to dumping by imposing countervailing or **antidumping duties** in order to protect domestic industry by neutralizing the effects of dumping. It perhaps is most difficult to demonstrate convincingly that sporadic or persistent dumping is injurious to the importing nation; development of cost-based evidence that dumping has occurred also is subject to abuse by governments in importing nations. Governments are most likely to respond vigorously to predatory dumping, especially if it occurs as a result of export subsidies provided by governments of exporting nations in order to gain an advantage in strategic industries.

Finally, as nations have negotiated reductions in tariff and quota barriers, a variety of other nontariff barriers have received increasing attention. Governments often create preferences for domestic producers by adopting **buy-national policies**, either in the form of rules that mandate purchases from domestic firms if their prices are no more than a certain percent higher than those of foreign firms, or through more informal administrative rules and practices that favor domestic firms. Such policies can have significant impacts on international trade, since government purchases often account for 30 percent or more of gross domestic product. Another example is governmental technical and administrative standards relating to factors such as health, safety, and the environment. Such policies are considered legitimate or acceptable if their primary intent is to achieve objectives such as health or safety; however, they are considered to be nontariff barriers subject to foreign challenge if their primary objective or effect is to shield domestic producers from more efficient foreign competitors.

KEY CONCEPTS AND TERMS (Define each concept, and briefly explain its significance.)

Nontariff trade barrier

Import quota

Global versus selective import quota

Tariff-rate quota, or two-tier tariff

Orderly marketing agreement

Voluntary export restraint (VER)

Trade diversion

Domestic content requirement

Domestic subsidy

Export subsidy

Dumping: price-based versus cost-based evidence

Predatory versus sporadic dumping

Persistent dumping and international price discrimination

Antidumping duties

Buy-national policies

Government procurement policies

Technical and administrative nontariff barriers

TRUE OR FALSE? (On an exam, be prepared to explain *why* the statement is true or false.)

T F 1. An import quota imposes a quantitative restriction on the volume of imports.

T F 2. Unlike a tariff, a quota does not cause the domestic price of the imported product to rise.

T F 3. A quota generally creates greater welfare losses for the importing nation than does a tariff, because the revenue that would have gone to the government with a tariff often is captured by the exporting firms when a quota is used.

T F 4. A tariff contributes to more rapid price increases over time than would a quota, as domestic demand rises.

T F 5. A voluntary export restraint avoids the domestic price increases and welfare losses caused by tariffs or quotas.

T F 6. Local content requirements protect domestic industry by discouraging the use of foreign parts or components.

T F 7. Government export subsidies increase export volume, but also tend to reduce export prices and increase domestic tax burdens.

T F 8. Export firms that practice international price discrimination are engaging in sporadic dumping.

T F 9. Predatory dumping is designed to strengthen market power or dominance by eliminating foreign competitors.

T F10. U.S. government incentives to promote "Buy-American" practices are simple acts of patriotism, and are not regarded as nontariff trade barriers.

MULTIPLE CHOICE

1. A global import quota
    a. specifies the quantity of imports allowed from each exporting nation
    b. ensures an even supply of imports throughout the year
    c. creates uncertainty about market access for individual exporting nations
    d. is much more common among industrial nations than is the use of selective import quotas

2. An import quota that reduces imports to the same level as would an equivalent ad valorem tariff will
   a. raise domestic prices by less than would the tariff
   b. avoid the redistributive effect of the tariff
   c. have a lower protective effect than would the tariff
   d. most likely generate less government revenue than would the tariff

3. A nation that uses an import quota rather than an import tariff to protect its domestic industry will find that over time, as demand for this industry's product increases,
   a. price will rise less rapidly than with a tariff
   b. price will rise more rapidly than with a tariff
   c. price will not change, because a quota is not a tax
   d. domestic output will rise less rapidly than with a tariff

4. In comparison with an import quota, a voluntary export restraint
   a. generates more government revenue for the importing nation
   b. avoids the price increases of an import quota
   c. creates potential export opportunities for nonrestrained suppliers
   d. is very difficult to revise or renegotiate over time as conditions change

5. A local content requirement
   a. reduces imports by specifying that a minimum percentage of a product's total value must be produced domestically
   b. is designed to maintain quality control for local production
   c. applies to domestic firms but not to factories owned and operated by foreign corporations
   d. is a new method for reducing nontariff trade barriers

6. A domestic subsidy to enable an industry to compete against imports
   a. avoids the protective effect of a tariff
   b. avoids the redistributive effect of a tariff
   c. avoids the deadweight consumer surplus loss of a tariff because it does not distort domestic prices
   d. raises the domestic prices of imported products

7. A nation that uses an export subsidy will find that
   a. its export prices will rise relative to import prices
   b. its export volume will increase
   c. its total revenue from export sales will necessarily increase
   d. it will be able to balance its government budget with fewer domestic taxes

8. A nation that reduces export prices to offset the effects of a domestic recession is engaging in
   a. persistent dumping
   b. predatory dumping
   c. sporadic dumping
   d. an orderly marketing agreement

9. A nation that enables an emerging industry to sell exports at prices below production costs in order to weaken foreign competition is engaging in
   a. persistent dumping
   b. predatory dumping
   c. sporadic dumping
   d. an orderly marketing agreement

10.   Nontariff barriers include all of the following except
       a.   a government-sponsored "Buy-American" policy
       b.   a corporate income tax
       c.   technical standards on product ingredients that tend to favor domestic products over
             imported products
       d.   policies for bidding on government contracts that exclude or discriminate against foreign
             producers

PROBLEMS AND SHORT ANSWER QUESTIONS

1.   Discuss the basic differences between import tariffs and import quotas as devices for restricting
       trade. If a nation wishes to implement quotas, what practical difficulties will it face in choosing
       between global and selective quotas?

2.   Use the following graph to answer the questions below.

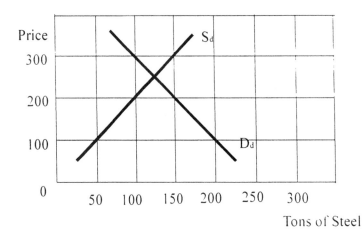

       a.   Assume that the world price of steel is $100 per ton, and that the United States imposes a
             40 percent tariff on steel imports. Show the effects on the graph. Now suppose instead
             that the United States imposes a quota on steel imports equal to the quantity that would
             be imported under the 40 percent tariff. Show and explain what would happen to the
             domestic price of steel in each case. Explain how the welfare effects of tariffs and
             quotas differ by comparing the individual effects (redistributive, protective, revenue, and
             consumption) in this example.

52

b. Focus now on the revenue effect of the tariff in this example. If a quota is used instead, explain how the disposition of this revenue depends on policies adopted by the domestic government and on the relative bargaining strengths of import firms and export firms. Why is this effect likely to be an additional welfare loss to the nation if it chooses to use a quota rather than a tariff?

c. In one year, suppose the demand for steel increases by 50 tons at each price, because of income growth. Draw the new demand curve on the graph. Show and explain what would happen to price, domestic output, and imports, first with the 40 percent tariff in place, and alternatively with the equivalent import quota in place. Explain why the price would rise with the quota, but not with the tariff.

3. What are orderly marketing agreements and voluntary export restraints? Why might an importing nation find these more politically acceptable than tariffs or quotas? Despite this, why might the importing nation suffer greater welfare losses from voluntary export restraints than from either tariffs or quotas designed to reduce imports by the same amount?

4. Consider the U.S. automobile market, where domestic sales of new cars are shared among domestic factories of both U.S. and foreign auto firms and factories abroad owned by both foreign and U.S. firms. Explain the meaning of a domestic content requirement, and why the U.S. government might institute such a requirement for the automobile industry. What would be the effects on domestic auto firms, on foreign auto firms, and on U.S. purchasers of new cars?

5. Consider the following graph, identical to that found in Question 1. Suppose that the U.S. government used a domestic subsidy equal to $40 per ton of steel to support the domestic steel industry, rather than using tariffs or quotas. Show the impact of this subsidy on domestic price, domestic output, and imports. Compare the effects of this subsidy with those of the 40 percent tariff analyzed earlier (redistributive, protective, revenue, consumption). Why does such a domestic subsidy bring less welfare loss to the nation than would a tariff? What would be a possible social justification for such a subsidy?

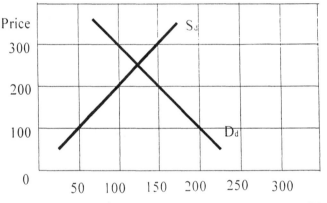

6. What is dumping? Why is it often so difficult to identify or measure? Why is it important to distinguish among the three different types of dumping, especially when a nation considers the potential use of antidumping or countervailing duties in response to dumping?

7.   Discuss the ways in which government procurement policies, "buy-national" campaigns or policies, and technical regulations adopted by national governments can constitute nontariff trade barriers. Why do you think these policies might be more difficult to deal with in international trade policy negotiations than are tariff and quota barriers?

EXPLORATIONS BEYOND THE CLASSROOM

1.   Review a recent World Trade Organization (WTO) annual report on national trade barriers to get a flavor of the extent to which individual countries use tariffs, quotas, and other nontariff trade barriers to restrict imports or to promote exports. Compare the reports on two or three industrial nations with those on two or three developing countries to get a sense of different trade barrier levels and relative reliance on tariffs and nontariff barriers.

2.   Locate recent newspaper articles (perhaps using newspaper or periodical indexes) dealing with claims of dumping. Can you determine which types of dumping are involved? Why might this not be clear? What action, if any, is the government of the importing nation taking or considering? What might be the effects of such action?

3.   In 2002 the U.S. steel industry filed complaints about injury suffered from excessive imports and alleged dumping practices by other nations, and the U.S. government responded by providing tariff relief. Consult newspaper articles and government documents to learn more about these complaints. How easy or difficult is it to determine which type of dumping might be involved in this case, and to decide how the U.S. government should respond?

4.   Locate recent newspaper articles dealing with government procurement policies, buy-national programs, environmental protection policies, or technical regulations that are being challenged as nontariff trade barriers. Why are these policies being challenged? What justifications do the governments provide for using such policies?

CHAPTER 7

TRADE REGULATIONS AND INDUSTRIAL POLICIES

SYNOPSIS OF CHAPTER CONTENT

This chapter moves beyond the economic analysis of tariffs and nontariff trade barriers developed in previous chapters to examine the actual trade policies and regulations that have been employed by the United States and other nations throughout history.

The first tariff legislation in the United States, passed in 1789, was designed primarily to achieve revenue objectives. This remained an important goal of tariffs through the early 1800s, but with industrialization and diversification of the U.S. economy the federal and state governments began to rely more heavily on income, property, and sales taxes as sources of revenue to finance government spending. Today tariffs constitute a negligible source of government tax revenue in the United States. In 1791 Alexander Hamilton presented his famous argument in support of tariffs to protect emerging U.S. industries. This classic **infant-industry argument** for tariffs motivated tariff legislation in the 1820s, and by that time the protective argument for tariffs was well established in the United States.

The average level of tariff protection has fluctuated significantly in the United States, reaching levels between 40 and 50 per-cent during the 1890s, falling to 27 per-cent with the trade liberalization movement of the early 1900s, and rising to a record 53 per-cent in 1930 as the **Smoot-Hawley Tariff Act** was passed by Congress and approved by President Hoover in an effort to protect the United States from the emerging economic depression. The Smoot-Hawley Act was futile and counterproductive, as other nations throughout the world responded with similar measures, either in retaliation or to protect their own economies, and the resulting collapse in world trade only prolonged and deepened the global economic depression of the 1930s.

The **Reciprocal Trade Agreements Act** of 1934 signaled a trend toward trade liberalization in the United States. This act of Congress granted authority to the President to reduce U.S. tariffs, provided that other important trading nations would reciprocally lower their tariffs on imports of similar goods. The **most-favored-nation (MFN)** clause also was incorporated, guaranteeing that each exporting nation would receive similar treatment to that of the "most favored" nation, thereby ensuring equal treatment for all exporters of any particular product. Presently, the United States grants MFN status to all but a handful of nations which are not included for various foreign policy reasons.

After World War II, most of the major industrial nations signed the **General Agreement on Tariffs and Trade (GATT)**, which established a framework and an international institution designed to promote nondiscrimination among nations in international trade, multilateral import tariff reductions, and elimination of import quotas except in specified circumstances. The United States was one of the original 23 signatories, and the GATT has expanded to include more than 100 member nations today.

In addition to its day-to-day surveillance of trade policies, the GATT membership has undertaken a series of specific "rounds" of multilateral trade negotiations. The **Tokyo Round**, completed in 1979 after 5 years of talks, achieved large percentage reductions in tariffs, but because tariff levels already had been reduced to relatively low levels the impact of these additional cuts was not significant. Of greater importance were the agreements to reduce a variety of nontariff barriers to trade, including arbitrary customs valuations procedures, health and safety standards that operated primarily to exclude imports, government subsidies and countervailing duties, restrictive licensing requirements, and government procurement practices that favored domestic suppliers or excluded foreign firms from bidding on government contracts. Benefits from the Tokyo Round perhaps were more limited and difficult to assess than those of earlier negotiations such as the Kennedy Round, both because tariffs already had been reduced to low levels and because agreements to reduce NTBs are more subjective, more difficult to monitor and verify, and more difficult to measure than is the case with tariffs.

In 1986, GATT members entered into the **Uruguay Round** of trade negotiations. As with the Tokyo Round, the focus was primarily on nontariff barriers. However, the goals were more ambitious, extending into areas not covered before. Protection of intellectual property relating to patents and copyrights was one objective, affecting products ranging from movies to medicine and computer software. Moving beyond the traditional focus on products to eliminate trade barriers against imports of services in areas such as transportation and finance was another goal. A major focus was on agriculture, with the United States pressing the European Community and other nations to end domestic subsidies, export subsidies, and import barriers that have been used to provide substantial support and protection for domestic farmers. Another objective was to increase the participation of developing nations in GATT talks and to recognize more effectively the special needs and circumstances of these nations. The Uruguay Round was scheduled to be completed by 1990, but intense disagreement, especially relating to agriculture, led many to fear that the negotiations would fail. The talks collapsed, deadlines were extended, and only at the last possible moment, in mid-December 1993, was agreement reached.

After ratification by GATT member nations, the Uruguay Round took effect in January 1995. This also transformed the GATT into the **World Trade Organization (WTO)**. While GATT was an accord among nations, the WTO is a more formal membership organization with a wider scope and greater authority than GATT. Experience during the coming months and years will determine the actual influence and effectiveness of this new institution for promoting freer trade among nations.

U.S. firms that export or compete with imports have access to various remedies if they believe that foreign competition is unfair or imposes undue hardship on them. The **escape clause** in U.S. trade legislation provides temporary relief for U.S. companies if it can be shown that the domestic industry is suffering serious injury, that imports are increasing, and that the imports constitute a substantial cause of the injury. In such cases it need not be shown that foreign firms or governments are engaging in "unfair" trade practices. In cases where export subsidies from foreign governments are deemed to provide unfair competitive advantages, the United States or other importing nations may impose **countervailing duties** to offset or nullify such advantages, under the terms of GATT. Such countervailing duties clearly offer protection for the domestic industry, although foreign export subsidies generally benefit the importing nation as a whole in the form of less expensive imports; thus, countervailing duties may not serve the best interest of society in the importing nation. Finally, antidumping legislation in the United States is designed to authorize duties or tariffs to offset any advantage gained by foreign firms that export products to the United States at prices below cost or below prices charged in their home markets. Again, injury caused by such dumping practices must also be demonstrated before antidumping duties may be imposed.

An additional trade policy tool used by the United States is Section 301 of the Trade Act of 1974, authorizing the United States Trade Representative to respond directly to trade practices of other nations that place "unreasonable" or "discriminatory" burdens on U.S. export firms. This unilateral track was established because of Congressional dissatisfaction with the often lengthy and ineffective multilateral resolution of trade disputes within GATT. Supporters contend that the mere threat of imposing Section 301 sanctions often induces other nations to eliminate unfair trade practices, while critics maintain that such forceful unilateral tactics violate the U.S. commitment to work through the multilateral channels that it accepted as a signatory to GATT.

Another subject of increasing attention in trade negotiations is the protection of intellectual property rights. Copyrights, patents, and trademarks traditionally have been used to protect such rights. When foreign firms imitate or produce a modified version of a protected product, without permission from or compensation to holders of copyrights or patents, they gain an unfair advantage. If they appropriate the trademark of another firm, they may gain sales unfairly and perhaps also damage the reputation of the trademark holder if their product is inferior to the original. The Omnibus Trade and Competitiveness Act, passed by the United States in 1988, provides more recourse or protection for holders of intellectual property rights, and the Uruguay Round of GATT trade negotiations also established more multilateral protection of such rights.

57

In contrast with measures intended to protect domestic firms from intense or unfair foreign competition, **trade adjustment assistance** is designed to facilitate a transition into other industries for companies and workers displaced by foreign competition. The rationale for such an approach is that if free trade and specialization according to comparative advantage increase the economic welfare of a nation, it is better to accept such gains and compensate specific groups who may lose from foreign competition, enabling firms and workers to move into areas in which the nation does have a comparative advantage. The alternative would be to protect and perpetuate jobs and investments in industries in which the nation is less efficient, thereby sacrificing the potential gains from free trade.

In recent years, a number of policymakers and analysts have urged the U.S. government to take a more assertive and proactive role in promoting domestic industry, responding in part to the perceived loss of U.S. competitiveness relative to other nations such as Japan and Germany. This approach, known as **industrial policy**, involves the use of specific incentives such as tax reductions, loan guarantees, low-interest government loans, and subsidies to fund research and infrastructure development. Although the U.S. government has intervened in the economy over the years to subsidize agriculture, support aircraft manufacturers and provide loan guarantees for auto firms, this runs counter to the prevailing free-market tradition of the U.S. economy. The U.S. government has not developed an explicit, comprehensive industrial policy designed to target support for specific industries or to promote "national champions." Other nations, especially France and Japan, have developed and implemented more formal and aggressive industrial policies. Whether government agencies such as Japan's **Ministry of International Trade and Industry (MITI)** have been successful in systematically picking winners is a topic of intense debate, as is the questions of whether such an approach would succeed in the United States.

One variant of industrial policy that has received growing attention since the 1980s is **strategic trade policy**. This relates to industries in which imperfect competition, rather than perfect competition, prevails. Industries with a small number of dominant firms, high fixed costs, and economies of large-scale production create conditions under which firms assisted by government subsidies can gain market share from foreign competitors, reduce unit costs, and capture benefits for themselves and their nation. High-technology industries, in which production experience or learning-by-doing reduces unit production costs, also would qualify as strategic industries deserving of government support. As with other forms of industrial policy, critics of strategic trade policy question the ability and political will of governments to pick industries carefully and successfully, and note also that strategic trade policy invites foreign retaliation and the risk of escalating government support and protection for industries.

The welfare effects of strategic trade policy are difficult to estimate and depend on the specifics of each case. In general, taxpayers in the nations using strategic trade policy to promote exports lose because of higher taxes to fund subsidies, export firms gain higher profits, and consumers in importing nations gain through lower prices resulting from the subsidies. However, if strategic trade policy succeeds in eliminating competition, the remaining dominant firm might well charge higher monopoly prices, with net losses to consumers.

Despite the debate over explicit industrial policy, it is clear that more general government support policies can significantly affect the international competitiveness of a nation's industry. Policies to increase saving and investment, to promote education, training, and research and development, and to provide competitive export credit terms as with the **U.S. Export-Import Bank** may serve to strengthen a nation's economy and thus enable its industry to compete against imports and succeed in export markets. Another advantage of this approach is that it does not invite the retaliation or charges of unfair trade policies that often result from the more interventionist industrial or strategic trade policies.

As the relative importance of the service sector in the U.S. economy has increased, trade policies relating to service exports have received growing attention. Although many services by their very nature cannot be exported or imported, others offer such potential. The United States has been a consistent net exporter of services, and has pressed its trading partners to reduce their barriers to service imports in industries ranging from banking and insurance to motion pictures and computer services. Trade barriers to service imports often are subtle and difficult to verify or measure, and protection of domestic services frequently is a socially and politically sensitive issue. Indeed, France and other EC nations have resisted U.S. efforts to reduce trade barriers in the motion picture industry, and ultimately prevailed in excluding this industry from the final agreement in the Uruguay Round of trade negotiations.

Finally, nations sometimes use trade policy not to protect or promote domestic industry but to impose **economic sanctions** on other nations in order to achieve certain foreign policy objectives. Such sanctions usually take the form of limiting exports from the sanction-imposing nation, limiting imports from the target nation, or controlling financial flows into the target nation. The economic impact of sanctions usually requires that they be imposed with multilateral cooperation rather than unilaterally by one nation, and even if they impose economic hardship their effectiveness in achieving the desired foreign policy objectives depends on generating a positive response from friendly government or private interest groups within the target nation rather than provoking a hardline response from an adversarial government with authoritarian domestic power. It should be recognized that, just as free trade is said to bring mutual gains to all parties, the imposition of sanctions generally brings welfare losses not only to the target nation but also to the sanction-imposing nation. Even if the sanctioning nation is willing to accept such losses, the historical record contains more instances of mixed results or failures than of clear successes in achieving the foreign policy objectives of economic sanctions.

KEY CONCEPTS AND TERMS (Define each concept, and briefly explain its significance.)

Smoot-Hawley Tariff Act

Reciprocal Trade Agreements Act

Most-favored-nation (MFN) clause

General Agreement on Tariffs and Trade (GATT)

Tokyo Round of GATT talks

Uruguay Round of GATT talks

World Trade Organization (WTO)

Escape clause

Countervailing duty

Section 301 of the 1974 U.S. Trade Act

Intellectual property rights

Trade adjustment assistance

Industrial policy

Export trading company

U.S. Export-Import Bank

Japanese Ministry of International Trade and Industry (MITI)

Strategic trade policy

Economic sanctions

TRUE OR FALSE? (On an exam, be prepared to explain *why* each statement is true or false.)

T F 1.   The initial tariff laws in the United States, established in the late 1700s, were established primarily to raise revenue.

T F 2.   In 1791, Alexander Hamilton advocated tariffs to protect new industries, using the infant-industry argument.

T F 3.   The Smoot-Hawley Act of 1930 was the first major effort in the United States to reduce tariffs and move toward free trade.

T F 4.   The most-favored-nation clause allows nations to preserve favored tariff treatment for historical allies.

T F 5.   The General Agreement on Tariffs and Trade, established in 1947, remains the primary international forum for negotiating trade agreements.

T F 6.   The Uruguay Round of GATT trade talks focused primarily on agriculture, services, and intellectual property.

T F 7.   The escape clause in U.S. trade law permits key industries to escape permanently the competitive effects of reduced trade barriers.

T F 8.   Countervailing duties are designed to promote fair trade by offsetting the effects of foreign export subsidies.

T F 9.   Strategic trade policy involves government targeting of key industries for export promotion, as MITI has done in Japan.

T F10.   Economic sanctions are most successful if imposed unilaterally, by a single nation.

MULTIPLE CHOICE

1.   The Smoot-Hawley Act of 1930
      a.   represented a turning point toward lower tariffs
      b.   represented the highest tariff levels in U.S. history
      c.   helped the United States recover from the Great Depression
      d.   prompted other industrial nations to reduce their tariff barriers against U.S. exports

2.   The rationale for a scientific tariff is to
      a.   provide revenue for the government
      b.   protect an infant industry against foreign competition
      c.   improve a nation's balance of payments
      d.   raise import prices to the extent that foreign production costs are lower than domestic costs

3.   The Reciprocal Trade Agreements Act of 1934
      a.   restricted the ability of the President to negotiate tariff reductions
      b.   made reductions in U.S. tariffs contingent on the willingness of trading partners to lower their tariffs
      c.   provoked a trade war that raised tariffs dramatically
      d.   eliminated the most-favored-nation clause in trade negotiations

4. Compared with the Tokyo Round, the Uruguay Round of GATT negotiations focused primarily on
    a. import tariff reductions
    b. government procurement policies
    c. trade in professional services and agricultural products
    d. product standards relating to health and safety

5. The escape clause is part of trade remedy law designed to
    a. provide temporary relief for workers and firms disrupted by reductions in tariffs or other trade barriers
    b. offset the effects of unfair trade practices in other countries
    c. help U.S. firms escape the effects of export subsidies provided by foreign governments
    d. retaliate against foreign firms that dump exports at prices below cost of production

6. A countervailing duty
    a. is the same as a scientific tariff
    b. protects firms from injury caused by foreign export subsidies
    c. is a retaliatory response to foreign tariffs
    d. is designed to generate revenue to offset a budget deficit

7. A Japanese government export subsidy would
    a. be beneficial to U.S. producers of similar products
    b. be harmful to U.S. consumers
    c. create an overall welfare loss for the United States, as U.S. firms would lose more than U.S. consumers would gain
    d. create an overall welfare gain for the United States, as U.S. consumers would gain more than U.S. firms would lose

8. U.S. industrial policy includes all of the following *except*:
    a. export financing from the Export-Import Bank
    b. nationalization of key industries such as steel
    c. tariffs to protect industries facing growing foreign competition
    d. legislation to allow for export trade associations

9. Strategic trade policy
    a. is used most frequently to support firms in perfectly competitive industries
    b. often involves subsidies and other support for high-technology firms in concentrated industries
    c. is practiced by only one major industrial nation today
    d. is designed to provide equal treatment for all industries

10. Economic sanctions against foreign nations are most successful
    a. if one major nation imposes them unilaterally
    b. when used against historical enemies rather than traditional allies
    c. when influential groups within the target nation support the objectives of the sanction-imposing government
    d. when the sanctions are harsh, comprehensive, and highly publicized

PROBLEMS AND SHORT ANSWER QUESTIONS

1. What motivated the United States to impose the record-high Smoot-Hawley tariffs in 1930? How did other industrial nations respond? What was the net impact on the global economy, and on each of the domestic economies involved?

2. How did the Reciprocal Trade Agreements Act represent a new direction for U.S. trade policy? What important role did the most-favored-nation clause play within this context?

3. What are the basic goals and principles of the General Agreement on Tariffs and Trade? How has its membership changed since its 1947 origin?

4. Compare and contrast the Tokyo Round and Uruguay Round of GATT multilateral trade negotiations, as each moved in different ways beyond a simple focus on import tariff reductions.

5.	In what ways do the international protection of intellectual property rights and the elimination of barriers against trade in services pose more subtle and difficult challenges than has been the case with barriers against trade in products?

6.	Explain how the escape clause, countervailing duties, and antidumping duties each serve distinct functions within the scope of U.S. trade remedy laws.

7.	Suppose that Brazilian firms can produce steel at a cost of $400 per ton, but that at this price U.S. steel firms can supply the entire domestic market, as shown in the following graph. If the Brazilian government provides a steel export subsidy of $50 per ton in order to gain a share of the U.S. market, show the effects on the graph. Identify the welfare gains and losses to different groups in the United States. Why does the U.S. government face a dilemma in deciding how, if at all, to respond to such a subsidy?

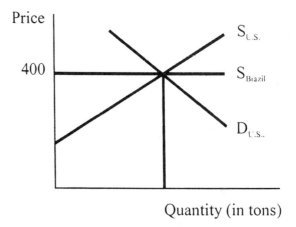

8.   What is the economic rationale for employing trade adjustment assistance rather than protective measures in response to dislocations caused by foreign competition? Why has adjustment assistance had only limited success in the United States?

9.   Compare and contrast the use of industrial policy by the United States with that of MITI in Japan. Why is there so much controversy regarding the advisability and effectiveness of industrial policy?

10.   Explain how strategic trade policy represents a specific form of industrial policy. Why is a national government tempted to provide subsidies for a strategic industry, and how does this create pressure for governments in nations with competing firms to provide similar subsidies? What are the strengths and limitations of strategic trade policy?

11.   If the U.S. government declined to use narrowly defined interventionist industrial or strategic trade policies but still wished to establish policies that would promote the global competitiveness of U.S. firms, what advice would you give?

12.   How and why do nations use economic sanctions to achieve various foreign policy objectives? What conditions must be met for such sanctions to be successful? Why do some observers believe that the Soviet grain embargo and the Iraqi sanctions were less successful than the sanctions against South Africa?

EXPLORATIONS BEYOND THE CLASSROOM

1.   Review and evaluate recent U.S. Congressional debate and testimony regarding the use of industrial policy and strategic trade policy. How does funding for the Export-Import Bank figure into this debate?

2.   What progress has been made in implementing Uruguay Round trade barrier reductions? What does our initial experience suggest about the future effectiveness and authority of the new WTO?

3.   Locate and discuss recent newspaper articles or government documents dealing with government subsidies, countervailing duties, and subsidies to strategic industries or firms such as Airbus and Boeing. What factors have contributed to Boeing's recent loss of market share to Airbus? How, if at all, do you think the U.S. government should respond?

4.   How do recent conflicts between Japan and the United States over strategic impediments to imports reflect the trade policy issues negotiated in the Tokyo and Uruguay Rounds?

5.   Locate recent articles dealing with the debate over economic sanctions against China for alleged human rights violations, and apply the criteria for successful sanctions to assess the probable impact of such sanctions against China.

CHAPTER 8

TRADE POLICIES FOR THE DEVELOPING NATIONS

SYNOPSIS OF CHAPTER CONTENT

As demonstrated in earlier chapters, international trade theory maintains that all nations can improve their welfare by specializing in production according to comparative advantage and participating in international trade to gain imports at a lower price than it would cost to produce them at home. We have not distinguished between developed and developing nations, but many analysts maintain that trade affects these two groups in different ways, and that the present international economic system actually works to the disadvantage of developing nations. This chapter examines the potential impact of international trade on developing nations, and explores policies designed to improve the economic conditions in these nations.

Developing nations differ from the more advanced, industrial nations in a number of important ways, although the most common single criterion used is to identify developing nations as those countries with per capita GDPs below a certain level. By this measure, a significant gap exists between the most advanced industrial nations with per capita GDPs of $25,000 or more and the poorest developing nations with per capita GDPs between $100 and $200 per year. Developing nations also tend to have more unequal income distributions, to be more agrarian, and to have higher infant mortality rates, shorter life expectancies, lower nutrition levels, and lower literacy rates than developed nations. Important exceptions exist, with some developing nations ranking much higher by quality-of-life indicators than by per capita GDP and others having high incomes yet few signs of human progress because of extreme inequality. In terms of international trade, developing countries tend to have higher ratios of exports to GDP than do most advanced nations, to trade more with industrial nations than with each other, and to depend heavily on exports of one or two **primary products** such as agricultural goods or minerals rather than having a more diversified export base.

One characteristic of primary products is that both supply and demand tend to be relatively price-inelastic. This means that small changes in quantity supplied, resulting for instance from good or poor growing conditions for agricultural products, create large price changes. Similarly, small swings in demand for minerals and other raw materials create significant price changes for these products. Thus, developing countries dependent on exports of one or two primary products are subject to very unstable export prices. Such price instability also may bring large fluctuations in export revenue from one year to another, particularly if the instability is caused by demand fluctuations that bring high prices and high quantities in good years and low prices and low quantities in poor years.

In addition to problems of short-term instability in export prices and revenues, developing countries also are said to suffer from declining or worsening **commodity terms of trade** over time. Critics contend that this arises both because demand of industrial nations for imports of primary products grows only slowly over time, as a result of low income-elasticity of demand for such products, and because exporters of manufactured products from developed to developing nations are able to exert monopoly power and maintain high prices for such manufactured exports. Thus, developing nations find that the prices of their traditional primary product exports relative to prices of their manufactured product imports fall over time. The consequence of these instability problems and worsening terms of trade is that the international trading system, according to such critics, is biased against the developing nations, with most of the anticipated gains from trade and specialization going, not to the developing nations, but rather to the advanced industrial nations.

A United Nations study in 1949 appeared to provide empirical support for this hypothesized deteriorating terms of trade for developing countries, but later reviews cast doubt on these results because of inadequacies in the gathering and interpretation of data. The theoretical support for declining terms of trade also was challenged by some analysts. Subsequent empirical studies have been inconclusive, some

67

showing no deterioration and others even a slight improvement in the terms of trade for developing nations from 1950 through 1970. Developing countries that depend on primary product exports suffered slightly declining terms of trade from 1974 through 1993, but the terms of trade for those with more diversified exports showed no significant trend during this period. Thus, the evidence is mixed, but concerns about vulnerability and instability from export price fluctuations remain strong.

Developing nations, working primarily through the **United Nations Conference on Trade and Development** (UNCTAD), have pressed the more advanced industrial nations for reforms in the international trading and financial system. Through these UNCTAD meetings, beginning in 1964 and convened every 4 years thereafter, the developing nations have called for a **new international economic order** that would be more supportive of their needs and interests. One element of their proposals or demands calls for international commodity agreements to stabilize primary product prices. Other elements seek trade preferences for exports of manufactured goods from developing nations, access to technology from advanced nations on reasonable terms, a more equitable share of the benefits from foreign investment, and more extensive and effective economic assistance from industrial nations.

Efforts to stabilize primary product prices through **international commodity agreements** often focus on **production and export controls** designed to stabilize export prices or revenues. In addition to such controls intended to adjust supply in response to fluctuations in demand in order to prevent price swings, international agreements often include the use of **buffer stocks** as management tools. Managers would purchase commodities and add them to buffer stocks during periods of surplus in order to prevent price reductions, and then sell from buffer stocks during periods of shortage to prevent prices from rising. The main challenge in administering buffer stock programs is to set target prices that are not so low as to deplete buffer stocks or so high as to require continual additions to large, unwieldy buffer stocks. An alternative approach to stabilization is the use of **multilateral contracts**, whereby importing nations commit to buying guaranteed quantities at a minimum price and exporting nations commit to selling guaranteed quantities at a specified maximum price. Such international agreements offer the potential for moderating the price fluctuations of internationally traded commodities, but conflicting interests between producers and consumers as well as management problems in setting and achieving target prices have made it difficult to sustain successful commodity agreements over extended periods of time.

Some developing countries, frustrated with the prospects for exports of primary products, turned toward an **import substitution** strategy for economic development. Such nations, particularly in Latin America, placed high tariffs on imports of finished manufactured goods, in an effort both to stimulate domestic production of such items and to alleviate balance of payments deficit problems. As shown in Chapter 5, even moderate nominal tariffs on final goods can create very high rates of effective protection if nominal tariffs on intermediate inputs are either lower or zero, so these import substitution policies did succeed in promoting domestic production. However, this production was not always consistent with comparative advantage, especially in industries characterized by economies of large-scale production, so import substitution often led to high-cost, inefficient domestic production for limited markets. These problems became more serious as countries also moved to promote domestic production of intermediate inputs, placing nominal tariffs on these items and then raising tariffs on the final products even further so as to preserve their effective protection.

To avoid the limitations of producing only for the domestic market with import substitution policies, other developing nations, particularly in Asia, used **export-oriented policies** to support export-led industrialization strategies. Although Hong Kong, Singapore, South Korea, and Taiwan did initially use protective measures to support domestic infant industries, they moved more quickly to reduce tariff protection and encourage globally competitive industries, building on their comparative advantages to promote exports of manufactured products rather than simply primary commodities. These countries experienced dramatic success with their exports of labor-intensive manufactured products, and have since shifted to incorporate more capital-intensive goods as their economies have developed. Many other countries that earlier pursued import substitution strategies have begun to move toward export promotion, but whether they can emulate the success of the Asian examples and whether the industrial nations will be receptive to growing imports of manufactured products from developing nations remains to be seen.

In order to support a more diversified export base for developing countries, the industrial nations were asked in the 1960s to deviate from the general principles of reciprocity and nondiscrimination and grant nonreciprocal, special tariff preferences to developing countries for their exports of manufactured products. Under the **generalized system of preferences (GSP)** program, beginning in the 1970s, industrial nations have selectively reduced or eliminated their nominal tariffs on imports of manufactures from developing nations. Each industrial nation has established its own GSP program, placing limitations on the volume of duty-free imports allowed from individual developing countries and excluding sensitive products from the program altogether. Because of limited coverage, and exclusion of sensitive labor-intensive items for which developing nations would have strong comparative advantages, the GSP programs to date have brought only modest benefits, and these have gone primarily to a small group of more advanced developing countries such as Mexico and more recently Malaysia.

A final topic that deserves mention in connection with trade and development issues is the **Organization of Petroleum Exporting Countries (OPEC)**. By establishing a cartel, OPEC was able to limit production and dramatically increase the price of oil exports, from $3 to $12 per barrel in 1973 and again in 1979 to levels above $30 and sometimes approaching $40 per barrel. Since the early 1980s, the OPEC cartel has found it more difficult to restrict global oil production, and purchasers have learned to economize or to utilize substitute energy sources, so world prices have fallen to levels as low as $12 per barrel recently. OPEC has demonstrated the potential for dramatic success as a cartel; however, it also illustrates the difficulty of sustaining a cartel as members seek to capture larger shares gains by expanding production, as producers outside the cartel enter the market or expand their production, and as buyers turn elsewhere. Although OPEC originally was touted as an example of how other developing nations could form cartels for exports of raw materials and extract their deserved rewards from the industrial nations, few if any other raw materials offer the potential for success that oil provided for OPEC. Furthermore, the disruptive and destabilizing impact of OPEC policies was in fact far more severe among the non-oil-producing developing countries than in the industrial nations such as the United States.

KEY CONCEPTS AND TERMS (Define each concept, and briefly explain its significance.)

Developing nations

Primary product exports

Declining commodity terms of trade

United Nations Conference on Trade and Development (UNCTAD)

New international economic order

International commodity agreements (ICAs)

Buffer stocks

Multilateral commodity contracts

Import substitution

Export-oriented development policy

East Asian tigers

Generalized system of preferences (GSP)

Organization of Petroleum Exporting Countries (OPEC)

TRUE OR FALSE? (On an exam, be prepared to explain *why* the statement is true or false.)

T F 1.   The most common, although imperfect, manner of distinguishing between developing and advanced nations is on the basis of per capita GDP.

T F 2.   Most developing countries acquire necessary primary products by importing them from advanced nations.

T F 3.   Many believe that developing countries have suffered from fluctuating and declining export prices.

70

T F 4.   Demand and supply conditions for primary products tend to be relatively price-inelastic.

T F 5.   The purpose of buffer stocks is to reduce or eliminate price fluctuations for primary commodities.

T F 6.   An example of import substitution would be for Peru to import automobiles from Japan rather than from the United States.

T F 7.   A generalized system of preferences is used to promote trade among developing countries.

T F 8.   UNCTAD is an organization that dramatically raised oil prices during the 1970s.

T F 9.   The East Asian tigers are newly industrializing nations that have used export promotion to achieve development.

T F10.   A cartel is able to achieve price increases for its exports primarily through its ability to control production.

MULTIPLE CHOICE

1.   Deteriorating commodity terms of trade refers to the contention that, for developing countries,
    a.   many of their export products deteriorate and cannot be stored well
    b.   prices of their primary product exports have fallen over time relative to prices of their manufactured imports
    c.   credit terms for borrowing from advanced nation banks to finance development have deteriorated over time
    d.   transportation charges for shipping their exports have risen over time

2.   Primary product prices tend to fluctuate significantly because
    a.   demand increases significantly as income rises
    b.   supply is highly elastic with respect to price
    c.   demand is highly elastic with respect to price
    d.   supply and demand are inelastic with respect to price

3.   The manager of an international commodity buffer stock would be expected to
    a.   purchase commodities when price exceeds target level
    b.   sell commodities when price is below target level
    c.   purchase commodities when price is below target level
    d.   sell commodities when inventories exceed target level

4.   Buffer stocks often have been excessive and costly to maintain because
    a.   target prices have exceeded equilibrium levels
    b.   target prices have been set lower than equilibrium levels
    c.   demand has grown faster than anticipated
    d.   managers get paid more for keeping large inventories

5.   Import substitution is a development strategy in which countries
    a.   begin to import from each other rather than from advanced nations
    b.   substitute newer products for those previously imported
    c.   use tariffs to promote domestic production of manufactured goods previously imported
    d.   use high taxes to discourage consumption of import goods

6. Export promotion is a development strategy in which countries
   a. try to create new markets for primary product exports
   b. seek aid from advanced nations to advertise their traditional export products
   c. use multilateral commodity contracts to stabilize export prices
   d. try to industrialize by supporting manufactured products in which they have a potential comparative advantage

7. The United Nations Conference on Trade and Development
   a. is a forum created by Germany, Japan, and the United States
   b. was established shortly after the end of World War II
   c. was established in the mid 1960s as a forum to lobby for a new international economic order
   d. is committed to developing more trade among the advanced industrial nations

8. The generalized system of preferences
   a. involves a selective reduction of industrial nation tariffs on imports of manufactured goods from developing nations
   b. is designed to improve the terms of trade for exports of primary products from developing countries
   c. is fully consistent with the GATT principles of reciprocity and nondiscrimination
   d. is designed to increase trade among developing countries

9. The term "newly industrializing countries" refers to
   a. a group of very low income nations in Africa
   b. a group of East Asian nations that have used export promotion strategies to support industrialization
   c. a group of Latin American nations that established their first industries in the 1990s
   d. all developing countries that were primarily agrarian nations until the 1990s

10. OPEC's ability to maintain a successful oil cartel depended on
    a. a highly elastic world demand for oil
    b. a highly elastic supply of oil from non-OPEC producers
    c. the ability of OPEC to enforce production cutbacks among its members
    d. a continuing recession among industrial nations after the initial OPEC oil price increase in 1973

PROBLEMS AND SHORT ANSWER QUESTIONS

1. Explain how the productive structures of many developing countries and the nature of supply and demand elasticities for primary commodities make these countries particularly vulnerable to export price fluctuations.

2. Show and explain how buffer stock management can be used to reduce the destabilizing effects of short-term supply or demand fluctuations for primary commodities. Why is the buffer stock approach unable to deal with problems of deteriorating terms of trade over longer periods of time?

3. Briefly outline the deteriorating terms of trade hypothesis for developing countries, and explain why the theoretical and empirical support for this view is inconclusive.

4.   Why did a number of Latin American countries turn to import substitution policies in the 1950s and 1960s? How did they employ trade policies to achieve these objectives? For example, if Peru imposed a 10 percent tariff on imported finished autos but no tariffs on imported auto components that account for 90 percent of the total value, calculate the level of effective protection that this tariff structure would provide for the assembly of autos in Peru (see Chapter 5 for review).

5.   How did the newly industrializing countries of East Asia use export promotion strategies to diversify their economies and achieve economic growth? How does this differ from traditional export promotion and from import substitution? Why does it appear to have been more successful than these alternatives?

6.   What is UNCTAD? How has it been used as a forum for promoting the call for a new international economic order, and why has this effort met with only limited success to date?

7.   What is the generalized system of preferences? What are its goals, and how would it support an export promotion development strategy? Why have the GSP programs of most industrial nations provided only limited benefits for developing countries?

8.   What trade policy reforms among the industrial nations would be required in order for the newly industrializing countries to experience continued growth with export promotion strategies and for other developing countries to be able to emulate this strategy successfully?

9.   What conditions were required for OPEC to succeed as a cartel? How did the success of OPEC during the 1970s and early 1980s set the stage for its apparent weakening since the mid 1980s?

10. What unique features of OPEC, including the nature of its export product and the cohesiveness of its members, make it unlikely that other groups of developing countries could achieve similar success by forming cartels to manage their primary product exports?

EXPLORATIONS BEYOND THE CLASSROOM

1. Locate recent newspaper articles dealing with the impacts of primary commodity price fluctuations on the economies of specific developing countries. Were these impacts negative or beneficial? Do you find any evidence that buffer stocks or multilateral contracts were used to affect these results?

2. Select a particular Latin American country and review recent economic news reports for indications of recent shifts from import substitution toward export promotion development strategies. What are the goals of such policy changes? What benefits have been realized? What problems or challenges have emerged?

3. Locate a recent economic news report on one of the East Asian newly industrializing countries. What indications do you find of continued export-oriented policies? Has the recent Asian economic crisis led such nations to change their outward-oriented development strategies?

4. Consult recent UNCTAD or other UN reports on the recent impacts of industrial nations on developing countries. How do the issues or concerns raised in these reports compare with the elements of the earlier new international economic order platform?

5. OPEC and oil prices remain in the news, as do concerns about potential future energy crises. Locate recent news articles dealing with OPEC and oil prices. Apply the conditions for a successful cartel outlined in the text to information in your selected articles to assess the current strength of OPEC.

6. Consult news reports on the consequences of China's admission to the WTO. Has China continued to open its economy on a broader level to international trade and foreign investment? To what extent have the concerns of those who opposed China's WTO membership been addressed?

CHAPTER 9

REGIONAL TRADING ARRANGEMENTS

SYNOPSIS OF CHAPTER CONTENT

Our earlier discussion focused first on the economic effects of free trade, and then on the consequences of trade restrictions such as import tariffs and quotas. We have analyzed the potential welfare gains of moving from protectionism to free trade, and also the reasons why nations often opt for restricted rather than completely free trade. Our implicit assumption has been that any nation that removed or reduced trade barriers would do so on a most-favored-nation basis according to the conditions of GATT (now the WTO), reducing specific tariffs equally on imports from all other nations. However, an alternative approach is for a small group of nations to form a **preferential trading arrangement**, reducing or eliminating tariffs on imports from member countries while retaining higher tariffs on imports from non-member nations.

This process of selective or limited trade liberalization is known as **economic integration**, also frequently called **regional integration** because most integration efforts involve countries within a single geographic region, often with common borders. Such integration is selective liberalization because it occurs in a world otherwise characterized by trade barriers and restrictions on movement of capital and labor, so the integration among members is accompanied by the continuing exclusion of non members.

Economic integration can take a variety of different forms, which also may be thought of as stages representing increasing degrees of integration. These stages often constitute a process through which member nations go as they move from limited to more comprehensive economic integration. The most limited form is a **free trade area**, within which members remove all tariff and nontariff barriers among themselves while allowing each member to retain its own trade barriers against non members. The European Free Trade Association (EFTA), established in 1960, is an example of this, as is the more recently negotiated North American Free Trade Agreement (NAFTA). A second stage is a **customs union**, in which members also agree to establish uniform tariffs on imports from non members; Benelux, formed in 1948, represents this form. A third stage of integration is a **common market**, which moves beyond a customs union to provide also for the free movement of resources (capital, labor) among the member nations. The European Community (EC), created in 1957, gradually phased in tariff reductions and met the terms for a free trade area by 1968, established the common external tariff required for a customs union by 1970, and has been eliminating barriers against factor mobility and thus moving toward a full common market since that time; thus, the terms "EC" and "Common Market" often are used interchangeably in reference to the European Community.

Economic integration might move even beyond these stages and evolve toward a full **economic union**. This involves the unification or harmonization of social, taxation, and fiscal policies at the regional level rather than retaining the more traditional national autonomy in these areas. Incentives or pressures for such harmonization arise in part because the free movement of capital and labor created by a common market makes it less feasible for member nations to conduct independent policies relating to taxation or social spending without causing frictions or undesired movements of labor or capital from one nation to another. For similar reasons, an economic union may also include a **monetary union**, whereby members establish a common currency at the supranational level in order to avoid the costs or problems associated with different interest rates, fluctuating exchange rates, and frequent conversion from one national currency to another to finance trade, travel, or investment.

The economic welfare implications of integration can be separated into the **static** or immediate effects and the **dynamic** or longer-term effects on economic growth and trade. The static or short-term effects may include two opposing dimensions, a welfare-increasing **trade-creation effect** and a welfare-reducing **trade-diversion effect**. In an example of two countries forming a customs union, trade creation automatically occurs whenever one member begins to import from another member nation a product that it had been producing domestically prior to the union, behind the protection of high tariffs. In this case, elimination of tariffs on trade between members brings a net welfare gain because the increase in consumer surplus from the lower price exceeds the loss in profits to domestic producers as they lose part of their market to producers in the other member nation. This gain includes a *production effect*, analytically equivalent to reducing the protective effect of a tariff as the tariff rate falls, and a *consumption effect*, comparable to reducing the deadweight consumer loss of a tariff when consumption increases as the tariff rate falls.

However, if a member nation begins to import from its partner a product that prior to the union it had been importing from an outside nation, trade diversion occurs. In effect, the nation is shifting its imports from an efficient outside nation to a less efficient producer in a member nation, which now has an advantage because it no longer must pay the tariff that still applies to imports from outside nations. Even in such cases where trade diversion occurs, there may be welfare gains for the member nation if the trade-creation effects resulting from a lower price to consumers and domestic producers are larger than the increase in the cost of imports to the nation resulting from the trade-diversion effect of shifting to a higher-cost partner producer. It should be emphasized that these welfare effects are being analyzed from the vantage point of the member nations; trade diversion obviously brings welfare losses to those outside nations whose producers lose export markets to less efficient producers within the union.

Whether the trade-creation effects are likely to outweigh the trade-diversion effects of a regional integration effort depends on a number of factors. Trade creation is more likely if the members have similar economic structures before the union but potentially quite different comparative advantages, so that the new trade generated among members will be economically efficient. A union among a larger number of countries also increases the likelihood that low-cost producers will be included among the members. A union with a low external tariff also reduces the risk of trade diversion, since low external tariffs make it less likely that inefficient internal producers will displace more efficient firms in nonmember countries.

In addition to these static effects, the dynamic effects of economic integration also must be considered. By expanding the size of the market unimpeded by trade barriers, members may benefit from lower prices as capital-intensive industries realize the lower costs from economies of large-scale production. Integration may also spur more intense competition among larger firms that previously had enjoyed some degree of monopoly power when operating in domestic markets behind protective trade barriers. Such competition may bring not only lower prices initially but also greater innovation over time. The increased income and enhanced competition associated with integration may also bring higher levels of investment and hence more rapid economic growth over time. These dynamic benefits may increase welfare not only for the member nations, but also for outside nations who may gain from expanding export markets even if they suffer initially from static trade-diversion effects.

Several historical examples illustrate the different stages of and approaches to regional economic integration. The **European Community** (EC) is perhaps the most successful, lasting integration effort we have seen. Created in 1957, the EC has expanded from its original 6 members to its current membership of 15 nations. Beginning with the Treaty of Rome, the EC liberalized internal trade and had established a free trade area by 1968. It had become a customs union by 1970 when a common external tariff was established. Although often referred to as the "Common Market," the EC made only limited progress toward the free movement of capital and labor among members until the mid-1980s, announcing in 1985 its "EC 1992" program for achieving resource mobility and for removing a variety of remaining nontariff barriers such as government procurement policies that were hindering trade among the members. At the Maastricht Summit in 1991, EC members established goals of moving toward monetary union with fixed exchange rates and eventually a common currency, other forms of more complete economic union, and more extensive political unification. Thus, the stage was set for the EC to move beyond a common market to become the **European Union** (EU).

These steps toward more complete union or "economic deepening" within the EU are occurring at the same time that the EU is considering steps toward "economic broadening" by extending its membership to include other groups of nations. Such groups might include the remaining members of the European Free Trade Area (EFTA) in Western Europe, a number of Mediterranean nations, and those Eastern European nations that have undertaken economic reforms in moving toward free market economies. Given the need for more extensive policy coordination as nations move toward more complete economic union, it remains to be seen whether economic deepening and broadening will be possible simultaneously for the EU.

One important feature of the EU is its **Common Agricultural Policy (CAP)**, in which it uses a system of **variable levies** or import tariffs to domestic agriculture, with the levies adjusted to equal the difference between domestic target prices and the (usually) lower world market prices for agricultural commodities. Surplus commodities purchased by EU governments to support domestic prices are either stored or sold on world markets with the assistance of EU **export subsidies**. The CAP, accounting for a significant share of the total EU budget, has generated friction within the EU as consumers in some member nations have subsidized inefficient farmers in partner nations. It also has been a major point of contention within the Uruguay Round of GATT negotiations as the United States, Japan (nations that historically also have protected and subsidized domestic farmers) and developing nations have sought to achieve freer international trade in agricultural commodities.

Although the United States has not participated in economic integration efforts until recently, it did enter into a free trade agreement with Israel in 1985, established a free trade area with Canada in 1989, and in 1993 extended this relationship with Canada to ratify the North American Free Trade Agreement with Canada and Mexico (NAFTA). The U.S.-Canada Free Trade Agreement is expected to provide larger benefits for Canada, because of its much smaller economy and the potential for economies-of-scale gains through exports to the United States, but smaller gains also are expected for the United States. NAFTA has been much more controversial, and is unusual in its attempt to integrate two large, industrial nations with a sizable but still much smaller developing country. The primary effects of NAFTA are likely to be felt by Mexico and the United States. Some in the United States fear the loss of domestic jobs as labor-intensive industries move to Mexico because of lower wage rates, and there are parallel concerns in Mexico about firms in more capital-intensive industries, once attracted by Mexico's import substitution policies, returning to the United States as tariffs are reduced. Although most analysts predict net job gains in both countries, each will face challenges of dislocation and adjustment as realignments according to comparative advantage take place.

Another area of concern is environmental. Mexico's lower level of economic development means that environmental regulations are either less stringent or less well enforced, leading some to predict that U.S. firms in industries with significant production pollution would move to Mexico to reduce production costs and thereby cause job loss in the United States and more serious pollution in Mexico. Other analysts recognize this risk but note that Mexico's environmental standards and enforcement will more quickly approach U.S. levels as NAFTA increases the level of economic development in Mexico. NAFTA also provides for freer movements of agricultural products, services, and financial services among members. Overall, Mexico as the smallest economy is expected to receive the greatest share of economic gains from NAFTA. The experience of the next few years with NAFTA may influence not only the level of commitment to this regional organization but also whether the call at the 1994 Summit of the Americas conference for the creation of a **Free Trade Area of the Americas (FTAA)** by the year 2005 is followed by meaningful action.

As with the earlier U.S.-Canada agreement, some fear that gains to NAFTA members will come partially at the expense of outside nations that lose export market share through trade diversion. Indeed, a general concern about preferential trading arrangements such as the EU and NAFTA is that, rather than being initial steps toward freer global trade, they may become inward-turning regional blocs that exclude outside nations through trade diversion and other restrictive measures. Such concerns usually do not arise with respect to preferential agreements among developing countries, such as the Central American Common Market (CACM) or the Latin American Free Trade Area (LAFTA). Member nations here stand to gain from more efficient industrialization through economies of scale, but internal and regional political difficulties and problems of equitably sharing the gains from integration among member nations have to date prevented regional integration efforts among developing countries from achieving stability and sustained progress.

Finally, East-West trading arrangements deserve brief comment even though they do not represent preferential arrangements such as the EU or NAFTA. Prior to the dissolution of the Soviet Union and the economic reforms in Eastern Europe, the central or command planning directed from Moscow created a type of preferential trading system within the Soviet bloc. The command planning system and the shortage of convertible currency meant that trade between the western market economies and the eastern bloc nations often took the form of **countertrade**, with products exchanged on a barter basis rather than on a cash payment basis. Foreign investment was limited, but often involved **coproduction agreements** between western firms and eastern state agencies, with firms again receiving payments or profits through such industrial cooperation agreements as a share of the output that they produced rather than as cash payments. With the Eastern European nations and former Soviet republics now moving toward greater reliance on the market system and private property ownership, opportunities for East-West trade and investment appear more promising, but the challenges of facilitating such trade and investment during this transition period remain considerable.

KEY CONCEPTS AND TERMS (Define each concept, and briefly explain its significance.)

Preferential trading arrangement

Free trade area

Customs union

Common market

Economic union (including monetary union)

Static effects of integration

Trade-creation effect

80

Trade-diversion effect

Dynamic effects of integration

European Union (EU)

Common Agricultural Policy (CAP)

U.S.-Canada Free Trade Agreement

North American Free Trade Agreement (NAFTA)

Asia-Pacific Economic Cooperation (APEC)

East-West trade, countertrade

TRUE OR FALSE? (On an exam, be prepared to explain *why* the statement is true or false.)

T F 1.   Preferential trading arrangements depart from the GATT principle of nondiscriminatory trade barriers.

T F 2.   Members of a free trade area agree to maintain identical tariffs on imports from nonmember nations.

T F 3.   A common market allows for free trade and unrestricted movements of labor and capital among members.

T F 4.   The EU and EFTA both are examples of customs unions in Europe.

T F 5.	Trade creation occurs if a country begins to import from another member of a free trade area a product that it had produced domestically before the union was formed.

T F 6.	Trade diversion occurs if a country begins to import from another member of a free trade area a product that it had imported from a non-member nation before the union was formed.

T F 7.	Trade creation and trade diversion represent dynamic rather than static effects of economic integration.

T F 8.	Economies-of-scale gains to Canada and Mexico, resulting from NAFTA, represent dynamic effects of integration.

T F 9.	A monetary union is likely to be one component of economic union, the highest stage of integration.

T F10.	Countertrade is the term used to describe trade among members of a free trade area.

MULTIPLE CHOICE

1.	A preferential trading arrangement with free trade among members and different external tariffs set by each member is
	a.	a free trade area
	b.	a customs union
	c.	a common market
	d.	an economic union

2.	A preferential trading arrangement with free trade among members, a common external tariff, and free movement of labor and capital among members is
	a.	a free trade area
	b.	a customs union
	c.	a common market
	d.	an economic union

3.	A preferential trading arrangement with free trade among members and a common external tariff is
	a.	a free trade area
	b.	a customs union
	c.	a common market
	d.	an economic union

4.	Suppose that Country A has domestic firms that could supply its entire market for Product X at a price of $10, while Country B firms could supply Product X at $8 and Country C firms at $6. If Country A initially has a 50 percent tariff on imports of Product X and then forms a free trade area with Country B,
	a.	trade creation and welfare gains for Country A will occur
	b.	trade creation and welfare losses for Country A will occur
	c.	trade diversion and potential welfare losses for Country A will occur
	d.	trade creation and welfare gains for Country C will occur

5.	In Question 4, suppose instead that Country A initially has a 100 per cent tariff on imports of Product X; if all other assumptions remain the same,
a.	trade creation and welfare gains for A will occur
b.	trade diversion and welfare gains for A will occur
c.	trade diversion and welfare losses for A will occur
d.	trade diversion and welfare losses for C will occur

6.	Potential dynamic effects of economic integration include all of the following except
a.	lower production costs because of economies of scale from serving a larger internal market
b.	trade creation because of importing from a more efficient partner country
c.	greater efficiency and innovation because of more intense competition among firms from all member countries
d.	a higher level of investment and more rapid economic growth

7.	The common agricultural policy (CAP) of the EU
a.	requires all EU members to produce a common set of agricultural products
b.	has reduced agricultural prices within the EU
c.	protects EU farmers with variable levies and uses subsidies to finance the export of surplus produce
d.	helps promote global free trade in agricultural products

8.	One historical example of movement toward a complete economic union is
a.	the EC Maastricht Summit of 1991
b.	the U.S.-Canada Free Trade Agreement
c.	the European Free Trade Association
d.	the European Coal and Steel Community

9.	The North American Free Trade Agreement calls for
a.	unrestricted labor migration between Mexico and the United States
b.	eventual free trade among Canada, Mexico, and the United States
c.	a common external tariff for Canada, Mexico, and the United States
d.	identical environmental regulations in Canada, Mexico, and the United States

10.	Trade between Eastern European nations and Western nations frequently includes all of the following features *except*
a.	countertrade or barter exchange
b.	coproduction agreements between Western firms and Eastern European firms or governments
c.	contract manufacturing agreements
d.	exports and imports financed by payment in hard currencies such as U.S. dollars or Swiss francs

PROBLEMS AND SHORT ANSWER QUESTIONS

1. Briefly outline the different stages of economic integration. What are the potential benefits of moving from one stage to the next? How does each successive stage require greater political cooperation or coordination among member nations?

2. Suppose that the graph below represents the domestic supply and demand for autos in Country A. Suppose also that firms in Country B supply exports at $10,000 per auto, and firms in Country C at $8,000 per auto. If Country A initially imposes a tariff of 50 per cent on imported autos and then forms a customs union with Country B, show and explain the static effects. Will trade diversion occur? Does economic welfare in Country A increase or decrease from this union? Explain.

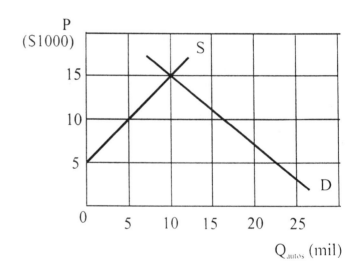

84

3.   Consider an example with the same initial conditions as in Question 2, but now assume that Country A forms a customs union with Country C instead of with Country B. Show and explain how the static efficiency and welfare effects are different in this case.

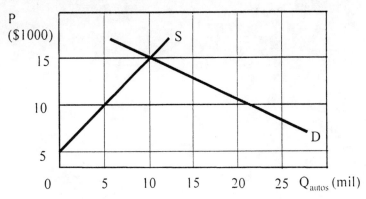

4.   Now consider an example with the same initial conditions as in Question 2, but assume that Country A initially had imposed a tariff of 100 percent on imported autos, rather than only 50 percent. Explain why the static effects include only trade creation in this case.

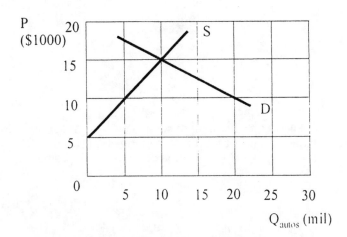

5. Briefly explain how the EU manages its common agricultural policy. How does the CAP create higher food prices for consumers within the EU, impose significant budget costs on the EU, and complicate GATT trade negotiations? Why is it difficult politically for the EU to modify or eliminate its CAP?

6. In what ways does NAFTA, which forms a free trade area among countries at quite different levels of development, pose more significant challenges than those faced by EU members when they began their integration process in the 1950s? Specifically, what are the potential gains and losses from NAFTA for Mexico and for the United States?

7. What are the potential dynamic gains from regional economic integration? How might these gains be significant for developing countries that form free trade areas, especially those that have pursued import substitution policies in the past?

EXPLORATIONS BEYOND THE CLASSROOM

1.   Consult recent journals, magazines, or newspapers for information on progress within the EU toward more complete economic union. What have been the initial results of currency unification and introduction of the Euro in January 1999?

2.   With the continuing economic reforms in Eastern Europe, what efforts are being made to include Eastern European countries as new EU members? Do there appear to be any conflicts or trade-offs between such "broadening" measures and the parallel efforts to "deepen" integration among the existing EU members?

3.   Review Congressional hearings and news accounts for information and analysis on how Mexico and the United States are dealing with the employment and environmental issues associated with the implementation of NAFTA.

4.   What progress, if any, is being made toward regional integration among Latin American nations? Is there continuing serious discussion about extending NAFTA to include such nations, as envisioned by the plans for FTAA? Is there evidence of other Latin American nations suffering from trade diversion as a result of NAFTA, losing export markets as the United States shifts to Mexico for imports?

5.   Locate articles reviewing the progress of MERCOSUR toward regional integration within Latin America. Who are the MERCOSUR members? What potential conflicts arise when countries such as Chile consider establishing free trade agreements with the United States or the European Union rather than with MERCOSUR nations?

6.   Consult recent International Monetary Fund publications to determine the extent to which EU members conduct international trade with each other rather than with outside nations. What has been happening to the total magnitude of EU imports from nonmember nations, and to such nations' share of EU imports?

7.   Locate articles dealing with the recent experience of Eastern European nations with the transition process toward market-oriented economies. How have their successes and difficulties affected their involvement in trade with other nations?

CHAPTER 10

INTERNATIONAL FACTOR MOVEMENTS AND MULTINATIONAL ENTERPRISES

SYNOPSIS OF CHAPTER CONTENT

So far we have accepted the standard assumptions of international trade theory, that productive resources can flow costlessly from one industry to another within a country but that only goods and services can flow from one country to another. In this chapter we consider the consequences of resources, such as capital and labor, moving across national borders. The factor-endowment theory of trade predicts that capital-abundant countries gain access to labor by importing labor-intensive products; an alternative would be for labor to flow from where it is relatively abundant and inexpensive to where it is scarce and expensive. Thus, international flows of capital or labor can be seen as substitutes for international trade in goods and services.

One important institutional form through which resources flow from one nation to another is the **multinational enterprise (MNE)**. Precise definitions vary, but there is general agreement that a multinational enterprise has ownership control (10 percent or more of voting stock) of production facilities located in several different countries. The unique feature of MNEs is that such production operations are integrated or coordinated on a global basis, rather than simply within an individual country. Most MNEs hold large shares of total assets and generate significant percentages of their revenues in nations other than the home countries of their parent companies.

Some multinational enterprises combine their operations internationally through **vertical integration**, as when petroleum companies invest abroad to acquire control of crude oil reserves or when manufacturing firms produce components in foreign facilities (backward integration). Other multinationals engage in **horizontal integration**, as when soft drink companies own subsidiaries in many countries to bottle and distribute their products. Finally, MNEs may engage in **conglomerate** expansion, constructing or acquiring foreign facilities in industries unrelated to their domestic operations, in which case their primary motivation would be to diversify and reduce risk rather than to integrate operations on a global basis.

What motivates firms to invest outside their home countries? The obvious answer is to seek profits, but this response does nothing to explain why firms invest abroad rather than at home to maximize profits. A more specific motivation is to gain access to foreign markets. Large foreign markets may be more efficient to serve through local production rather than by exporting from the home country, as illustrated in an intermediate stage of the product life cycle model. This helps explain much investment of U.S. firms in Western Europe and Canada, which represents a significant share of total U.S. direct foreign investment. A variation of this would be the manufacturing operations of U.S. firms in many Latin American nations, made profitable by import substitution policies that place high tariffs on imported manufactured products in order to stimulate domestic production.

A second motivation is to gain access to natural resources. This explains the vertical integration of U.S. oil companies that invest in extractive operations in the Middle East or Venezuela, or the investments of copper companies in Chile. Many of the Asian investments of Japanese enterprises also follow this pattern. The objective is to gain secure sources of raw materials and to achieve the efficiencies from internally coordinating vertically integrated activities.

A final motivating factor is to reduce production costs by taking advantage of factors ranging from climatic conditions for agricultural activities to low labor costs for labor-intensive manufacturing activities. Indeed, MNEs may shift production facilities abroad during the latter stages of the product life cycle, often simultaneously introducing newer, more capital-intensive products in their home countries. In such cases, favorable tax treatment by host nation governments may contribute to these cost advantages.

In deciding how to supply a foreign market, an enterprise may first export directly from its home market. This is reflected in one of the early stages of the product life cycle model. Once the foreign market becomes established and begins to expand, foreign production may be more effective than exporting. At this point the firm must decide between direct foreign investment and the licensing of a domestic firm within that foreign market. If the market is relatively small, licensing may be more cost-effective, whereas if the market is sufficiently large, the parent company may be able to take advantage of economies of scale and directly establish a foreign production facility. Additional factors such as unique features of a foreign culture, host country government restrictions, and the extent to which foreign operations can be relatively independent rather than closely integrated with other global operations will influence whether an MNE chooses to invest abroad through a joint venture with a local firm or government agency rather than to establish a wholly-owned foreign subsidiary.

The United States most frequently is thought of as a home country for MNEs, but in recent years the United States has become a significant host country for MNEs from other nations. In some years foreign firms have invested more in the United States than U.S. MNEs have invested abroad. Critics have focused often on the rapid growth of Japanese investment in the United States, coming about in part because of the much higher saving rates in Japan than in the United States; yet several other nations have more direct foreign investment in the United States than does Japan. The United States traditionally has been open to free flows of capital across national borders, and foreign firms generally receive **national treatment**, operating under the same tax, labor, antitrust, and environmental laws as do domestic firms. One important exception is that foreign investment in the United States is limited in industries with national security considerations, as is true in most other countries.

An important example of recent foreign investment in the United States is the assembly plants of Japanese auto firms, commonly known as **transplants**. The motivation for such investment includes a desire to mute U.S. criticisms of excessive Japanese auto exports to the United States, to avoid actual and potential future barriers to exports from Japan to the United States, to gain greater access to the U.S. market as theorized in the product life cycle model, and finally to achieve lower production costs in comparison with cars produced in Japan as costs rose in Japan and as a lower yen/dollar exchange rate increased the dollar cost of Japanese exports. Assessing the welfare impacts for the United States resulting from these transplants is extremely difficult, depending critically on assumptions about what would have occurred in the absence of such investments. Transplants bring new managerial and production technology to the United States and motivate U.S. firms to improve their efficiency. On the other hand, they import more parts or components from Japan than do comparable U.S. auto firms, and have lower labor costs because of slightly lower wage rates and significantly lower fringe benefits.

International joint ventures also have occurred in the auto industry. One example is New United Motor Manufacturing, Inc. (NUMMI), with ownership shared equally by General Motors and Toyota. NUMMI owns and operates a formerly idle GM plant in Fremont, California, sourcing roughly 50 percent of components for its cars from Japan. Such joint ventures create welfare gains if they provide productivity improvements through collaboration that would not be available to either partner operating alone. NUMMI provided an opportunity for GM to learn more about Japanese managerial and production technology, and for Toyota to learn more about producing and marketing autos in the United States. Critics feared that NUMMI would create job losses for U.S. auto workers, but again this assessment depends on what would have occurred in the absence of the joint venture. NUMMI clearly has achieved significant production efficiencies in comparison with both low-technology and high-technology domestic GM auto plants.

The operations and activities of MNEs have generated intense debate, with some analysts identifying the benefits that MNEs bring and others focusing on the negative impacts and conflicts created by MNEs, especially within the host nation. Although many dimensions of this debate are reflected in the discussion of foreign investment in the United States, most of the attention has gone to the impacts of U.S. MNEs operating abroad.

Much of the controversy centers on employment effects. Some in the home country worry about job loss as MNEs move abroad, while others in host nations contend that job creation may be minimal if MNEs purchase existing firms or bring managers from their home countries. An example is the **maquiladora** plants located on either side of the U.S.-Mexico border, facilitated by a special bilateral program which allows duty-free shipment of components from U.S. plants to their counterpart plants in Mexico and the re-export of processed products back to the United States with import duties paid only on the value added in Mexico; critics in the United States complain about the loss of U.S. jobs, while those in Mexico assert that development benefits are limited because of low wages and adverse working conditions. Overall, evidence on employment impacts is mixed and, although U.S. MNEs do create domestic jobs as they develop new products at home while moving older facilities abroad, it appears to many that MNEs generate more rapid and painful labor market adjustments as they carry out global realignments of production operations.

Another set of concerns relates to national sovereignty. MNEs may have more resources and flexibility than domestic firms to avoid or evade policies of host nation governments, leaving such governments feeling more vulnerable to foreign influence. At the same time, MNEs may find themselves under conflicting pressures from two sovereign host and home nation governments, especially in areas related to foreign policy and national security. MNEs are expected to be responsible corporate citizens within the host nation, but often are criticized for trying to influence such governments.

The impact of MNEs on both the home and host nation **balance of payments** (discussed in the next chapter) also is a source of controversy. For the home nation, the outflow of capital to finance foreign investments has a negative balance of payments impact, although exports of materials, equipment, and components (as with the Japanese auto transplants) have positive impacts. Later repatriation of profits earned abroad also improves the home nation's balance of payments. The concerns of the host nation are a mirror image of these factors, with the initial capital inflow creating a positive balance-of-payments impact but later repayment of profits, interest, and royalties bringing offsetting costs. Again, the net effects are very difficult to estimate. However, unlike some aspects of MNE behavior that may bring global benefits shared by both home and host countries, the balance of payments for all nations must add up to zero, so it is not possible for the operations of any single MNE to create net balance-of-payments benefits for *both* home and host nations.

Taxation of MNE activities raises additional questions. The U.S. government permits U.S. MNEs to claim a **foreign tax credit**, reducing their tax liabilities to the United States by the amount of taxes paid to governments of host nations. This is designed to protect MNEs from paying more taxes to the U.S. government than they would if all operations were domestic, but some critics maintain that this provision is too lenient and that foreign tax payments should be deductible only from taxable income, not from taxes owed. A related provision of the U.S. tax code allows MNEs to **defer** payment of taxes owed to the U.S. government until foreign earnings are repatriated to the United States. Thus, a U.S. MNE that allows foreign subsidiaries to retain their profits abroad effectively is receiving an interest-free loan, perhaps indefinitely. Establishing tax treatment of U.S. MNE operations that is both equitable from a domestic perspective and also allows such MNEs to compete with firms from other home nations that provide more lenient tax treatment for their MNEs is a complex task.

Finally, governments frequently raise concerns about the **transfer pricing** policies of MNEs. Transfer prices are the prices at which MNEs transfer goods or services from a subsidiary in one nation to a different subsidiary in another nation. The ability to manipulate or alter transfer prices is a unique feature of globally integrated MNEs. Whereas most export firms prefer high prices for their products or services, import firms at the other end of the transaction bargain equally hard for low prices; there is a general presumption that prices on such internationally traded items reasonably reflect production costs, unless one firm has excessive market power. However, with a multinational enterprise such pricing decisions are internal to the firm, made at headquarters so as to maximize global corporate profits or welfare; prices on products or services provided by one subsidiary to another are bookkeeping or "transfer" prices, not market prices established between firms in competitive markets. Thus, the MNE would have an incentive to set a low transfer price on an item shipped from a subsidiary in one country to a second subsidiary in another nation in order to shift profits to the second firm if tax rates were higher in the first nation, or to reduce payment of ad valorem import duties in the second nation, or to evade the effects of profit repatriation restrictions in the first nation. Tax laws in most nations require MNEs to set prices at "arm's length," as if they were dealing with a separate firm, so transfer price manipulation is illegal; however, since most products or services transferred within MNEs are non-standardized, differentiated items, it usually is very difficult to determine that "arm's length" transfer pricing was not followed by an MNE. Taxing authorities maintain vigilance, and often share information with each other to help detect illegal transfer pricing policies.

The existence of multinational enterprises constitutes an interesting challenge for international trade theory. On the one hand, by transferring information and technology among nations, MNEs give more realism to the standard "perfect information" assumption of most trade theories. MNEs also provide a conduit for production to shift quickly and efficiently from one nation to another as comparative advantage shifts through the stages of the product life cycle theory. However, by moving resources such as capital and technology from one nation to another, the MNE is at odds with the standard trade theory assumption of resource immobility among nations. By contributing to more equal resource endowments among nations the MNE would appear to reduce the potential benefits from trade based on comparative advantage, but as long as technology is dynamic and changing the MNE is likely to be an important institution for facilitating both international trade and the international transmission of technology.

Another important phenomenon that represents a departure from standard international trade theory is **migration**, or the flow of labor from one nation to another. In a simple economic model, labor is expected to migrate from countries where it is abundant and wages therefore are low to countries where wages are high because of relative labor scarcity. When labor moves from where marginal labor productivity is low to where it is higher, global efficiency and total world output will increase. Such labor migration also has distributional effects. Labor scarcity is reduced in the country of immigration, wages will fall, and for similar reasons wages will rise in the country from which labor is migrating. This tendency toward wage equalization creates relative gains for the remaining workers and losses for owners of capital in the country from which labor migrates, and has opposite effects in the receiving country. Governments often impose severe restrictions on immigration for such reasons, although an alternative approach would be to realize the global gains from international migration and address the distributional impacts through domestic transfer programs. Immigration issues in the real world, of course, are more complex, in part because workers are not identical but have different levels of ability, training, and skill.

A specific problem arising from these differences is the **brain drain** phenomenon, whereby highly trained workers from developing countries migrate to more advanced industrial nations rather than remaining at home and contributing to the development of their home nations. Policies of governments such as the United States actually encourage this, by granting immigration permits more readily to highly trained workers than to unskilled workers. Solutions might include adjusting such immigration policies, restricting emigration of such skilled workers from their home countries, taxing their income earned abroad to recover the cost of training and education, and reforming educational programs to provide training more relevant to the needs of the home country.

International labor migration poses challenges to trade theory similar to those created by the MNE. International trade provides a means for a labor-scarce country to address this labor shortage by importing labor-intensive products from a labor-abundant nation. Alternatively, allowing labor to migrate will directly alleviate this labor shortage, and in the extreme case will eliminate the potential gains from international trade by equalizing resource endowments among nations. Thus, trade and labor migration can be seen as substitutes for each other; restrictions on international trade increase the pressure for immigration, and freer trade policies reduce such pressures by tending to equalize wages among nations.

KEY CONCEPTS AND TERMS (Define each concept, and briefly explain its significance.)

Capital and labor mobility

Multinational enterprise (MNE)

Vertical, horizontal, and conglomerate integration

Direct foreign investment

Motivations for direct foreign investment

Licensing agreement

International joint venture

Transplant

Maquiladoras

Foreign tax credit, tax deferral

Transfer pricing

International migration

Brain drain

TRUE OR FALSE? (On an exam, be prepared to explain *why* the statement is true or false.)

T F 1.   Most international trade theories assume that labor and capital cannot flow from one country to another.

T F 2.   Multinational enterprises are defined as firms that *export* to six or more different nations.

T F 3.   The ownership by General Motors of an auto plant in Mexico is an example of vertical integration.

T F 4.   MNEs in capital-intensive industries most likely would choose licensing over direct foreign investment when expanding into relatively small foreign markets.

T F 5.   Japanese auto firms established transplants in the United States primarily to gain access to inexpensive raw materials.

T F 6.   U.S. firms established maquiladora plants primarily to gain access to the Mexican consumer market.

T F 7.   Transfer price manipulation occurs when MNEs alter prices of items shipped internationally from one subsidiary to another in order to reduce global tax payments.

T F 8.   MNEs from the United States and other advanced nations invest almost exclusively in developing countries, because of low wage rates.

T F 9.   International migration of labor tends to increase wage gaps between nations and to reduce global economic efficiency.

T F10.   The term "brain drain" refers to problems experienced by developing countries when some of their skilled, highly trained people migrate to industrial nations for more lucrative employment opportunities.

MULTIPLE CHOICE

1.   A multinational enterprise (MNE)
     a.   is a firm whose stockholders come from several nations
     b.   is a firm that exports to several different nations
     c.   is a firm with production facilities in several nations
     d.   tends to be smaller than the largest domestic firms in its home country

2. Horizontally integrated MNEs invest abroad primarily to
   a. gain access for their products to foreign markets
   b. gain access to raw materials such as oil and copper
   c. achieve lower production costs
   d. diversify their operations into new product areas

3. A direct foreign investment by IBM to produce components for personal computers sold in the United States is an example of
   a. horizontal integration
   b. vertical integration to increase production efficiency
   c. conglomerate expansion
   d. a licensing agreement

4. MNEs might enter into international joint ventures for any of the following reasons except to
   a. comply with host country government restrictions
   b. deal more effectively with different language and cultural dimensions
   c. gain access to technology or managerial skills
   d. achieve close coordination among global production facilities

5. Concerns about employment impacts of MNE investments
   a. relate primarily to job loss in the home country
   b. relate primarily to job loss in the host country
   c. relate more to short-term employment disruption than to longer-term or permanent net job loss
   d. tend to be less serious in industries characterized by strong labor unions and collective bargaining

6. The probable impact of MNE activity on the home or source country balance of payments is
   a. initially negative, because of capital outflows, but later positive because of profit repatriation
   b. initially positive, but later negative
   c. positive in both the short term and the long run
   d. negative to the extent that MNE investment generates outflows of materials, equipment, and other products

7. An MNE would have a financial incentive to increase the transfer price of exports from a foreign subsidiary to its parent company if
   a. tax rates are higher in the host country than in the home country
   b. import tariffs are high in the home country
   c. the host country government restricts profit repatriation
   d. tax rates are higher in the home country than in the host country

8. The primary motivation for locating maquiladora plants along the U.S.-Mexico border is to
   a. gain access to natural resources in Mexico
   b. benefit from conglomerate expansion
   c. reduce production costs because of lower-wage Mexican labor
   d. sell products in Mexico without paying import tariffs

9. Labor migration from one country to another
   a. intensifies the differences in relative resource endowments among nations
   b. leads to international convergence of wage rates and to greater global economic efficiency
   c. raises wage rates in the country to which workers migrate
   d. increases the potential for international trade based on comparative advantage

10.   The tendency for well-educated and highly skilled workers to migrate from developing countries to industrial nations is
       a.   part of the maquiladora problem
       b.   part of the transfer pricing problem with MNEs
       c.   referred to as the "brain drain" problem
       d.   prevented by current U.S. immigration policy

PROBLEMS AND SHORT ANSWER QUESTIONS

1.   How would you define a multinational enterprise? If the manufacture of a particular product shifts from the United States to another country as predicted by the product life cycle model, under what circumstances would it be produced by a U.S. MNE rather than by an indigenous firm in that country?

2.   If a domestic firm decides to expand into global markets, briefly outline the important considerations as it decides whether to export, license a producer in a foreign country, enter into a joint venture with a foreign firm, or establish a fully-owned foreign production facility as an MNE.

3.   What different reasons or motivations might enable a domestic enterprise to internationalize by expanding into foreign production operations? How does the distinction between vertical and horizontal integration enter into this analysis?

4.   For many years Mexico pursued an import-substitution development strategy, but recently has entered into a free trade agreement with the United States and Canada, through NAFTA. Explain how and why some U.S. MNEs might have incentives to return their production facilities to the United States, while others would have new incentives to relocate to Mexico as a result of NAFTA.

5.   Suppose that the United States has a corporate income tax rate of 50 percent and that Saudi Arabia has a tax rate of 30 percent. If the subsidiary of a vertically integrated MNE earns a profit of $100,000 from its extractive operations in Saudi Arabia, calculate the taxes that would be paid to each government under current U.S. tax law. Now calculate how taxes paid to each government and total taxes would change if the U.S. foreign tax credit provision were eliminated, and U.S. MNEs could deduct foreign taxes paid only from their U.S. taxable income rather than from their U.S. tax obligation.

6.   Briefly explain the concept of transfer price manipulation and why MNEs have the potential for such behavior. Return to the example of Question 5. Given the U.S. tax deferral provision regarding foreign earnings, explain whether this MNE would have a tax incentive to raise or to lower the transfer price of crude oil shipped from a subsidiary in Saudi Arabia to a refinery subsidiary in the United States. How would this affect global taxes paid, and distort reported profits in each country? Would either country gain extra tax revenues from this manipulation?

7.   Explain the potential beneficial and adverse impacts of MNEs on employment, in both home and host countries. Why is it often so difficult to estimate accurately such short-term and long-term employment effects?

8.   Suppose that the following graphs represent labor market conditions in Mexico and the United States. If labor were permitted to migrate between the two countries. show and explain the consequences for wage rates in each country and for total output between Mexico and the United States. Would global economic efficiency improve or deteriorate? What conflicts would such migration pose in Mexico. and in the United States? How would free trade between Mexico and the United States affect the pressures or incentives for labor migration?

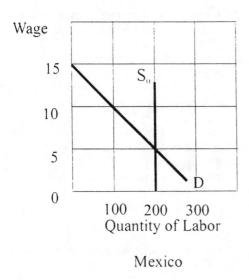

Mexico

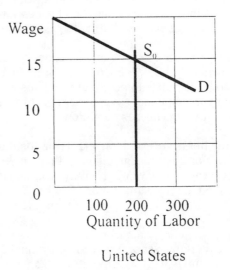

United States

9. Explain the "brain drain" phenomenon. If you were economic advisor to the president of a developing country, what policies would you recommend to resolve problems in this area?

EXPLORATIONS BEYOND THE CLASSROOM

1. Consult recent U.S. government publications (e.g., *Survey of Current Business*) to determine recent trends in direct private foreign investment. How much have U.S. MNEs invested abroad in recent years? How does this compare with investments of foreign firms in the United States? What are the total values of outstanding U.S. direct foreign ownership abroad, and of foreign ownership in the United States? Which countries are the major sources of recent investments? Which countries account for the largest shares of outstanding foreign ownership of U.S. assets?

2. Consult recent newspapers or magazines for articles dealing with controversies over foreign investments of U.S. MNEs, or over direct investments of foreign MNEs in the United States. Do these conflicts relate to potential problems in the home country, or in the host country? Do the issues involve national sovereignty concerns, employment impacts, taxation, transfer pricing, or balance-of-payments considerations?

3. Do some library research on an international joint venture between a U.S. firm and a foreign enterprise or government, either in the United States or in another country. What does each partner bring to this venture? Why would neither the U.S. firm nor the foreign enterprise have undertaken the investment alone? What benefits does this collaboration appear to provide? What conflicts or challenges do the partners appear to have in terms of working effectively together?

4. Explore the same set of issues in Question 3 as they apply to the recent merger between Daimler-Benz AG and Chrysler Corporation, each a large multinational enterprise in its own right.

5. Consult recent news sources or Congressional documents for discussions of immigration to the United States. Do the motivations for immigration correspond to the economic factors discussed in the text? How difficult or easy is it to distinguish between economic and social or political motivations for immigration? Do you find evidence of brain drain dimensions? What government policies for dealing with these immigration issues are being applied or considered?

CHAPTER 11

THE BALANCE OF PAYMENTS

SYNOPSIS OF CHAPTER CONTENT

Previous chapters have dealt primarily with the real side of international economics, exploring such topics as comparative advantage, export and import activity, trade policies, and international movements of labor and capital through forms such as migration or the activities of multinational corporations. In this chapter we shift to the financial side of international economics, beginning with a discussion of the balance of payments and later turning to topics such as foreign exchange markets, balance-of-payments adjustment mechanisms, international debt problems, and potential reforms of the international monetary system.

The **balance of payments** is a financial record of transactions between residents of one country and the rest of the world. The balance of payments is a *flow* statement, showing the volume of funds flowing into and out of a country over a specified period of time, usually 1 year. Transactions are recorded using a double-entry accounting system, in which **credits** represent receipts of payments by foreigners and **debits** represent payments by residents to foreigners. Thus, from a U.S. perspective, credits could arise from exports of merchandise, purchases by foreign tourists in the United States, or investments made by foreign corporations in the United States. Alternatively, debits could arise from imports of merchandise, U.S. tourist expenditures abroad, U.S. foreign aid, or foreign investments made by U.S. corporations.

Many different formats are used to present balance-of-payments statements, one of which is as follows:

Balance of Payments, 1999

Current Account
      Merchandise trade (exports minus imports)
      Services trade
      Income receipts and payments
      Unilateral transfers

Capital and Financial Account
      Short-term capital flows
      Long-term capital flows
            Portfolio investment
            Direct foreign investment
      Statistical discrepancy
      Official reserve asset flows

Merchandise trade, the first item of the **current account,** includes the monetary value of all **goods** that a nation exports or imports, with exports having a plus or credit impact because they create an inflow of funds from abroad. The **services** category includes a variety of items, ranging from tourist expenditures to transportation services. Income receipts and payments includes income from foreign investments and compensation of employees stationed abroad. Again, transactions that involve payments from foreigners have a plus or credit impact, while those involving payments to foreigners have a negative or debit impact on the current account. **Unilateral transfers** involve one-way transactions, as the name implies, and include such items as U.S. aid to other countries, gifts from U.S. residents to people or institutions in other countries, and remittances from immigrants in the United States to relatives in their home countries; each of these examples appears as a negative or debit entry, whereas payments in 1991 by some foreign governments to the U.S. government to share the financial expense of the Gulf War had a significant positive or credit impact on the unilateral transfers account.

Capital and financial account transactions also appear with plus signs or as credits if they involve the flow of funds into the United States, and with negative signs or as debits if they involve outflows. Thus, foreigners depositing funds in U.S. banks to benefit from higher interest rates in the United States than abroad will have credit impacts, contributing to a capital account surplus. Foreigners acquiring long term bonds issued by U.S. corporations or the U.S. government are making **portfolio investments**, also having a credit impact. Acquisition of financial assets with maturities of 1 year or less is considered to be a **short-term capital** transaction, while the sale or acquisition of assets which mature in more than 1 year is recorded as a **long-term portfolio** transaction. **Direct foreign investment** is another component of the long-term capital account: construction or acquisition by U.S. multinational corporations of plants in other countries would involve outflows in this category, with debit or negative impact, while investments of foreign MNCs in the United States would have the opposite impact. Firms that acquire ownership interests of less than 10 percent in a foreign corporation are considered to be making portfolio investments, while ownership of 10 percent or more of a foreign company's stock is considered to be enough to exercise management control, and thus is regarded as direct foreign investment. Finally, the **statistical discrepancy** item reflects the reality that balance-of-payments data collection and analysis are incomplete and imperfect, with some transactions simply estimated, some improperly recorded and others undetected and omitted completely. This category is included within the capital account because short-term capital flows generally are the most frequent sources of errors and omissions. The amount recorded is a residual, calculated so as to make total credits equal total debits. A credit or plus entry indicates a net inflow of unrecorded capital, while a debit or negative entry signifies a net outflow of unrecorded capital to other countries.

Official reserve asset flows sometimes are included in the capital account, but also may be recorded separately. If the U.S. government gives up gold or hard currencies such as the German mark in exchange for dollars held by foreign governments, this is considered as an "export" of reserves and recorded as a plus or credit transaction; it creates an inflow of dollars, just as would exports of goods or services. Such reserve flows, sometimes referred to as **official settlements transactions**, can be thought of as the mechanism by which nations pay for balance-of-payments deficits or gain reserves as a result of balance-of-payments surpluses.

Although individual transactions often are described as having either credit or debit impacts, because balance-of-payments accounting is a double-entry bookkeeping system each transaction actually has both a credit and a debit side. For instance, a U.S. export to Japan that was paid for by a deposit to the Tokyo bank account of the export firm would be recorded as an export credit on the current account and as a debit on the short-term capital account because of the increased financial claim of the U.S. firm against a Japanese bank. Similarly, a U.S. aid contribution to Somalia would be shown as a debit on the current account (a unilateral transfer) and as a credit on the short-term capital account because of the increased financial claim of Somalia against the United States. Because each credit entry has an equal debit entry, the overall balance of payments always balances or equals zero. However, a balance calculated for only those items that appear on the current account or the short- and long-term capital accounts may well show the value of debit entries to exceed that of credit entries, in which case the nation would be said to have a balance-of-payments **deficit**. The financing of this deficit by giving up reserves through an official settlements transaction would create the offsetting credit entry, as the excess foreign holdings of the nation's currency flowed back into the country.

A nation's balance-of-payments statistics are reported in a variety of ways. For instance, the **merchandise trade balance** for the United States, reflecting exports and imports of products, shifted from a small surplus in 1970 to a deficit of nearly $150 billion in 1986, narrowing slightly since then. The U.S. balance on **services** rose from a small surplus in 1970 to levels above $50 billion by the 1990s, meaning that its **goods and services balance** showed smaller deficits than did the trade balance alone. Finally, since in most years the United States has a unilateral transfers deficit, its **current account balance** has shown larger deficits than on goods and services alone. The current account balance also is referred to as the **net foreign investment** of a nation. For instance, a current account surplus generates an inflow of funds that can be used to acquire assets abroad or to reduce liabilities to foreigners. Thus, the capital account deficit that mirrors a current account surplus represents an outflow of funds used to purchase foreign assets. Similarly, a current account deficit is accompanied by negative net foreign investment, or by increased foreign ownership of assets within the nation.

A focus on any single balance may be misleading. For instance, although persistent U.S. current account deficits may tend to be viewed negatively, they may simply be the necessary reflections of the desire of foreigners to invest in the United States through short-term and long-term capital inflows. In this case, the U.S. current account deficits would be offset by capital account surpluses. It also is important to recognize that transactions recorded in one account may generate activity on other accounts later. For instance, U.S. aid would initially be recorded as a debit on the unilateral transfers account, but later might be used to pay for exports from the United States, which would create an offsetting credit on the merchandise trade account. Foreign investments by U.S. MNEs would initially create a debit entry on the long-term capital account, but later might generate current account credits through exports to foreign subsidiaries on the merchandise trade account and through profit repatriation on the service account.

Whereas the balance of payments is a *flow* concept, a related statement showing the **international investment position** of a nation is a *stock* concept. This statement for the United States shows the total value of assets in other nations owned by U.S. residents relative to the total value of assets in the United States owned by foreigners, at a particular point in time. Sometimes called the **balance of international indebtedness**, this statement shows a nation to be a **net creditor** if its claims on foreigners exceed the claims of foreigners on assets within its borders, or a **net debtor** when the reverse occurs. The United States shifted from being a debtor nation in its early years as a nation, reflecting borrowing from European investors, to becoming a strong creditor nation as U.S. firms and individuals invested abroad. However, the United States rapidly changed from a net creditor position of $337 billion in 1983 to a net debtor position of $871 billion in 1996. A nation's international indebtedness changes each year by the amount of its net capital inflows or outflows as shown on the balance of payments. Thus, the rapid emergence of the United States as now the world's largest debtor nation reflects the significant net capital inflows during the 1980s and 1990s. Those who view this development in positive terms see it as a desire and willingness of foreigners to invest in the United States, and thus a sign of confidence in the U.S. economy. Those who view our net debtor status with alarm see this negative net foreign investment as a side-effect of persistent U.S. trade deficits in recent years, and as a debt that eventually must be repaid--sooner rather than later if foreign investors lose confidence in the U.S. economy.

KEY CONCEPTS AND TERMS (Define each concept, and briefly explain its significance.)

Balance of payments

Double-entry accounting

Current account

Capital and financial account

101

Merchandise trade

Services

Unilateral transfers

Short-term and long-term capital flows

Direct foreign investment

Statistical discrepancy

Official reserve assets

Official settlements transactions

Merchandise trade balance

Balance on goods and services

Current account balance

Net foreign investment

Balance of international indebtedness

Net creditor or net debtor status

TRUE OR FALSE? (On an exam, be prepared to explain *why* the statement is true or false.)

T F 1.   The U.S. balance of payments shows the flow of dollars into and out of the United States during a given year.

T F 2.   Exports of wheat from the United States would be recorded as a capital and financial account credit on the U.S. balance of payments.

T F 3.   Imports of autos from Japan would be recorded as a current account debit on the U.S. balance of payments.

T F 4.   Deposits by Japanese citizens in U.S. banks to earn high interest would be recorded as a short-term capital and financial account credit on the U.S. balance of payments.

T F 5.   Aid from the United States to Somalia would be a unilateral transfer, a debit on the current account of the U.S. balance of payments.

T F 6.   A nation with a current account surplus would also have positive net foreign investment in other countries.

T F 7.   Official settlements transactions are used by governments to finance balance-of-payments deficits.

T F 8.   A nation always is required to pay for a merchandise trade deficit by giving up official reserve assets.

T F 9.   The balance of international indebtedness is another name for a nation's balance of payments.

T F10.   A nation would need a current account surplus in order to reduce (improve) its net debtor position.

MULTIPLE CHOICE

1.   A credit on the U.S. balance of payments will result if
      a.   U.S. churches donate food and clothing to people in drought-plagued India
      b.   a British resident receives dividends on her General Motors stock
      c.   a U.S. high school student spends money while studying for a semester in Japan
      d.   Sony of Japan purchases computer software from Microsoft of the United States

2. A debit on the U.S. balance of payments will result if
   a. a Mexican firm pays back its loan to a U.S. bank
   b. U.S. investors collect dividends on their Japanese treasury bills
   c. Lloyds of London sells an insurance policy to Chrysler Corporation
   d. Toyota of Japan constructs an automobile assembly plant in Kentucky

3. The U.S. balance of payments impact of a $3,000 payment by an immigrant farm worker in the United States to family members in Mexico would be
   a. a credit on the unilateral transfers account
   b. a debit on the unilateral transfers account
   c. a debit on the short term capital and financial account
   d. zero, because it was from one family member to another

4. The U.S. balance of payments impact of a $5 million profit repatriation payment by a subsidiary of IBM in France to its parent corporation in the United States would be
   a. a credit on the unilateral transfers account
   b. a debit on the short term capital and financial account
   c. a credit under income receipts and payments, on the current account
   d. zero, because the transfer was within IBM

5. The capital and financial account of the balance of payments includes all of the following *except*
   a. direct foreign investment
   b. purchases and sales of government securities
   c. bank loans to foreign corporations
   d. dividends and interest received from foreign investments

6. A current account balance-of-payments surplus implies an
   a. excess of exports over imports of goods and services
   b. excess of imports over exports of goods and services
   c. excess of exports over imports of goods, services, and unilateral transfers
   d. excess of imports over exports of goods, services, and unilateral transfers

7. An outflow of official reserve assets would be recorded as a
   a. current account credit
   b. merchandise trade balance debit
   c. capital and financial account credit
   d. unilateral transfers credit

8. The difference between a nation's balance of payments and its balance of international indebtedness
   a. is equal to official reserve transactions
   b. occurs because of foreign exchange rate fluctuations
   c. reflects statistical discrepancies
   d. reflects the difference between flow and stock concepts

9. A nation's net foreign investment position will worsen or decline if it's balance of payments shows a
   a. current account deficit
   b. current account surplus
   c. goods and services account deficit
   d. goods and services account surplus

10.   A nation that wants to reduce its net indebtedness to other nations would be advised to
        a.   reduce the foreign investments of its own MNEs
        b.   increase its foreign aid to other countries
        c.   reduce its holdings of official reserve assets
        d.   reduce its merchandise trade deficits

PROBLEMS AND SHORT ANSWER QUESTIONS

1.   What is the basic difference between the current and the capital and financial accounts of the balance of payments? Since the balance of payments is a double-entry accounting system, give an example to explain how an export of a Boeing jet from Seattle could have both a credit impact on the current account and a debit impact on the capital account of the U.S. balance of payments.

2.   For each of the following transactions, indicate which account on the U.S. balance of payments statement would be affected, and whether the primary entry would be a credit or a debit.

        a.   U.S. citizens pay $100,000 for Hondas produced in Japan.

        b.   A Japanese company pays $2 million to build an electronics factory in California.

        c.   U.S. students studying for a semester in Japan spend $300 at a restaurant in Tokyo.

        d.   Willamette University students give $500 to support relief efforts in Honduras after Hurricane Mitch.

        e.   Japanese citizens put $25,000 in U.S. banks to earn higher interest than they could earn in Tokyo banks.

        f.   A German subsidiary of a U.S. corporation repatriates $600,000 in profits to its headquarters office in Chicago.

        g.   U.S. citizens purchase $30,000 of 30-year bonds issued by a Mexican telecommunications firm.

3. Explain how a U.S. balance-of-payments deficit could lead to a loss of official reserve assets for the United States. If this reserve transaction were to be included in the overall U.S. balance of payments, explain why the overall balance would be zero.

4. What is the difference between the merchandise trade balance and the current account balance? Why is neither of these balances necessarily a good indicator of the basic strength or health of the U.S. balance-of-payments position?

5. Explain the various factors that make it necessary to include a statistical discrepancy category in the balance of payments accounts. Why is this usually included as part of the capital and financial account?

6.	Explain the connections between the current account of the balance of payments and the balance of international indebtedness for a nation. What has caused the United States to shift from a creditor nation to a significant debtor nation within the last decade?

EXPLORATIONS BEYOND THE CLASSROOM

1.	Consult recent U.S. government documents to review trends in the balance of payments over the past 10 years. What has been happening to particular categories such as the merchandise trade balance and the current account balance? What shifts do you observe regarding individual items such as investments of U.S. corporations abroad, and investments within the United States of foreign corporations? What conclusions, if any, can you reach regarding the basic "health" of the U.S. balance of payments?

2.	Review recent balance-of-payments reports for Japan and for the United States (consult International Monetary Fund publications). How do these reports help you to understand and evaluate the ongoing trade policy friction between these two nations?

3.	Analyze the U.S. balance-of-payments statements from 1990 through the present. Try to identify from these statements the year in which nations such as Germany and Japan made payments to the United States to cover some of the Gulf War costs. In which account does this appear? How does such an event make it very misleading to consider only the current account as a measure of a nation's trade balance?

4.	Consult recent U.S. government documents to review trends in the international investment position of the United States since 1980. To what extent has the United States changed from a creditor nation to a large debtor nation? What factors appear to have contributed to this change? In what ways is the situation of the United States as a debtor nation different from that of other debtor nations such as Mexico and Brazil?

CHAPTER 12

FOREIGN EXCHANGE

SYNOPSIS OF CHAPTER CONTENT

The **foreign exchange market** is the institutional arena in which people exchange one currency (usually their domestic currency) for the currency of another nation in order to finance international transactions. An individual in London may exchange pounds for dollars in order to pay for electronics products imported from the United States. A corporation in Tokyo may exchange yen for dollars in order to finance an automobile factory in Kentucky. The Japanese government may exchange yen for dollars in order to purchase U.S. government Treasury bills. Most such transactions involve the transfer of bank deposits rather than the literal trading of one currency for another, often handled electronically. The foreign exchange market exists not in a single physical location, but wherever financial institutions are prepared to exchange national currencies for each other. Large foreign exchange markets exist in London, New York, and Tokyo, supplemented by countless others, so that by phone one can complete a foreign exchange transaction at any hour of the day. Most foreign exchange transactions involve commercial banks, dealing with their commercial or individual customers, with their overseas branches, or through foreign exchange brokers with other banks.

The most common foreign exchange transaction is a **spot transaction**, an outright purchase of a foreign currency for immediate delivery. Although a spot transaction would be appropriate for financing an imminent delivery of imports, a firm that has arranged for delivery of a seasonal product 3 months from the present may enter into a **forward transaction** to exchange one currency for another at a rate specified today but taking place on a date 90 days into the future. This enables the firm to avoid the uncertain impact of exchange rate fluctuations while delaying the acquisition of foreign currency until it is needed for import payment. A third type of foreign exchange transaction is a **currency swap**, whereby a bank exchanges one currency for another with a second bank in order to obtain temporary access to a currency that it does not own, and agrees to reverse the transaction sometime in the future, at a rate specified today. This enables each bank to gain access to a currency for which it has a temporary need, without incurring the risk of exchange rate fluctuations when it wishes to reconvert back to its original currency.

Foreign exchange trading in 1995 averaged $244 billion daily, more than half of which were in spot transactions and one-third in swap agreements. The U.S. dollar was involved in more than 80 percent of the transactions, followed at some distance by the German mark and the Japanese yen, then the British pound and the Swiss franc. The major banks that make markets in foreign exchange earn profits on the **spread** between the **bid rate** at which they agree to acquire a currency and the **offer rate** at which they agree to sell it. For instance, with a bid rate of $.5851 per mark and an offer rate of $.5854, the spread would be $.0003 per mark, and a bank that simultaneously bought and sold 1 million marks would earn a profit of $300. Foreign exchange dealers in these banks also may attempt to earn profits by increasing their holdings of currencies that they expect to *appreciate* in value, and to sell or decrease their holdings of currencies that they expect to *depreciate*. Although such foreign exchange speculation offers the potential for large profits, it is highly risky and also can generate large losses and even threaten the survival of the participating bank; because of this, banks often impose trading volume limits on their foreign currency dealers.

In addition to the spot and forward markets, foreign exchange also can be bought and sold in the **futures market**. Unlike spot and forward transactions, futures trades occur in specific geographic locations such as the **International Monetary Market** of the Chicago Mercantile Exchange. Only a few major currencies are traded in the futures markets, with contracts limited to standardized amounts or volumes and available for delivery only on particular quarterly dates. Thus, the futures market lends itself more to currency speculation, while the forward market allows for contracts to be tailored to specific export or import needs. More recently, **foreign currency options** have become available, in which an individual

108

pays for the right to either buy (a **call option**) or to sell (a **put option**) foreign currency at a specified price or exchange rate. Such options may be attractive to firms bidding on major international contracts, enabling them to avoid exchange rate risk if the bid were successful without actually acquiring the foreign exchange that they would not need if the bid were not accepted. Of course, options also allow institutions or individuals to speculate on foreign exchange rate movements, risking only the price of the option in exchange for greater potential gain.

Beyond knowing the different ways in which foreign exchange transactions can be made, it is important also to understand how equilibrium exchange rates between two currencies are determined, and what factors cause these rates to change. For instance, from a U.S. perspective if one were to think of the demand for pounds as foreign exchange and the dollar/pound exchange rate as the price of pounds, U.S. demand for pounds would derive from the desire of U.S. residents to import products from Britain or to make investments in Britain. The demand curve for pounds would be downward-sloping, as are most standard demand curves, because an appreciation of the dollar (a reduction in the dollar/pound exchange rate) would increase U.S. demand for imports from Britain because of the lower dollar prices, and thus would increase the quantity of pounds demanded in order to pay for those increased imports. If the U.S. demand for imports were very inelastic or unresponsive to price changes, the U.S. demand curve for pounds would be correspondingly steep or inelastic. Alternatively, if U.S. demand for imports were highly elastic or responsive to price changes, the U.S. demand curve for pounds would be much flatter or more elastic.

By similar reasoning, the British supply of pounds would derive from the desire of British residents to import products from or to make investments in the United States. From this perspective, an appreciation of the dollar (a decrease in the dollar/pound exchange rate) would make British imports from the United States more expensive in pound prices, reducing the quantity demanded of such imports. If the British demand for imports were highly elastic or responsive to price changes, the quantity demanded would fall in percentage terms by more than the pound price increased, and the British supply of pounds would decrease as the dollar appreciated. However, if the British demand for imports were inelastic, the quantity demanded would decline only slightly, by less in percentage terms than the pound price increased, in which case the British supply of pounds would actually increase as the dollar appreciated. Thus, although the supply curve for pounds has the normal positive slope if British demand for imports is elastic, it becomes a downward-sloping or backward-bending curve if such demand is inelastic.

If the dollar/pound exchange rate were above its equilibrium level and the supply of pounds exceeded the demand at that rate, this would signify an excess supply of pounds or a British balance-of-payments deficit. A fall in the exchange rate (a depreciation of the pound) would be expected to restore equilibrium, as the quantity of pounds demanded increased and the quantity supplied fell. As we will explore further in a later chapter, such a depreciation will not necessarily restore equilibrium, especially if British demand for imports is unresponsive to price changes and the supply curve for pounds slopes downward rather than upward.

Although bilateral rates such as the dollar/pound exchange rate may be important for certain purposes, it often is useful to know in more general terms how a country's currency value is changing. The dollar's **effective exchange rate** is calculated as a weighted average of the exchange rates between the dollar and the currencies of U.S. trading partners, with weights equal to each partner's share of total U.S. trade. Thus, changes in the effective exchange rate indicate general movements of the dollar relative to the currencies of U.S. trading partners, with a fall or depreciation of the dollar reflecting an improvement in international competitiveness of U.S. products. Since inflation also affects the competitiveness of a nation's products, the **real effective exchange rate** captures this influence by adjusting the nominal effective exchange rate for the differential between the U.S. inflation rate and the weighted average of inflation rates experienced by our most important trading partners.

Internal consistency among exchange rates is ensured through a process of **arbitrage**. Two-point arbitrage, or the purchase and sale of one currency for another simultaneously in different financial centers, ensures for instance that the dollar/pound exchange rate is essentially the same in all markets.

109

Triangular or three-point arbitrage also can be used to ensure for instance that the dollar/pound exchange rate, the pound/mark exchange rate, and the mark/dollar exchange rate are consistent with each other. Any inconsistent alignments would enable an arbitrager to exchange dollars for pounds, pounds for marks, and then marks back into dollars for a low-cost and riskless profit, and such arbitrage trading would automatically create exchange rate adjustments bringing these rates into alignment with each other.

What is it that determines the relationship between spot and forward foreign exchange rates? A foreign currency is said to be at a **premium** in the forward market if the forward rate exceeds the spot rate, and at a **discount** if the reverse is true. As explained earlier, one reason to purchase foreign exchange in the forward market is to **hedge** against the risk of the exchange rate fluctuating between the time one decides to import a product and the time when one must make payment. Thus, a U.S. firm importing products from Japan in one month could hedge against a potential dollar depreciation by purchasing yen in the forward market. Conversely, a U.S. export firm that will be receiving payment in foreign currency would wish to hedge against a potential appreciation of the dollar.

Because the alternative to a forward contract is to wait and purchase yen in the spot market when the transaction occurs, the forward rate is considered to be a consensus forecast of what the spot rate will be at the time the forward contract matures. One reason why a foreign currency might be at a premium in the forward market is anticipation of domestic inflation that would be expected to depreciate the domestic currency relative to foreign currencies. Another factor influencing forward rates is the difference between domestic and foreign interest rates. Investors engage in **interest arbitrage** when they move funds into foreign currencies in order to take advantage of interest rates abroad that are higher than domestic interest rates. In order to avoid the exchange risk between the dates of purchase and maturity of the foreign financial asset, the investor would enter a forward contract to sell the foreign currency maturity value of the asset in exchange for his or her domestic currency. This process of **covered interest arbitrage** continues to push down the forward rate of the foreign currency relative to its spot rate until this **forward discount** is just equal in percentage terms to the percentage differential in interest rates between the two countries, eliminating any guaranteed profits from simply shifting funds to the high interest rate country. Thus, from this standpoint the difference between spot and forward exchange rates would be expected to reflect interest rate differentials. In practice, this does not always occur because some arbitrage is **uncovered**, governments engage in exchange controls, and speculation also influences spot and forward rates.

While hedging is designed to avoid the risk of foreign exchange rate movements, shifting the risks to those willing to accept them, speculation in the foreign exchange market involves an active assumption of risk in order to profit from exchange rate movements. Most speculation occurs in the forward rather than the spot market, because then funds need not be committed immediately. Speculators who take a **long position** in the forward market agree to purchase a forward contract, betting that the forward rate is not an accurate predictor of the future spot rate and that the spot rate will have risen to a level higher than the forward rate by the time the contract matures, creating an opportunity to sell the acquired foreign currency on the spot market and make an immediate profit. Speculators who take a **short position** in the forward market, agreeing to sell in the future a foreign currency that they do not presently own, are betting that the future spot rate will be lower than anticipated, enabling them to purchase at a low price on the future spot market and immediately make a profit by fulfilling their forward contract sale at a higher price.

Speculation is **stabilizing** if speculators tend to bet against market forces that cause exchange rate fluctuations, thus moderating such fluctuations. However, when speculators bet that initial fluctuations will continue in the same direction, they act to reinforce currency appreciations or depreciations and their speculation is then said to be **destabilizing**, intensifying rather than reducing disruptions to international trade and investment. Thus, whether currency speculation serves a useful social function remains an open question, with the empirical evidence ambiguous. It also should be noted that profit from such speculation is desired but by no means guaranteed; the risk is real, and news articles frequently recount the speculative losses of highly trained and skilled financial officers of banks and nonfinancial corporations.

KEY CONCEPTS AND TERMS (Define each concept, and briefly explain its significance.)

Foreign exchange market

Spot, forward, and futures foreign exchange markets

Foreign currency swaps

Bid rate, offer rate, and spread

Equilibrium exchange rate

Nominal and real effective exchange rate

Currency appreciation

Currency depreciation

Two-point and three-point arbitrage

Hedging

Covered and uncovered interest arbitrage

Foreign currency put and call options

Foreign currency speculation

Stabilizing and destabilizing speculation

TRUE OR FALSE? (On an exam, be prepared to explain *why* the statement is true or false.)

T F 1. The foreign exchange market is the place where internationally traded products are exchanged.

T F 2. If the foreign exchange value of the dollar goes from 110 yen to 100 yen, the dollar has depreciated in value against the yen.

T F 3. An appreciation of the dollar normally would be expected to reduce a U.S. trade deficit.

T F 4. A U.S. auto dealer agreeing to pay yen for autos to be imported in 3 months might want to hedge this contract by selling yen in the forward market.

T F 5. If the rate of inflation is higher in the United States than in Japan, the dollar would be expected to sell at a discount in the forward market relative to the spot market.

T F 6. If interest rates are higher in Europe than in the United States, the euro would be expected to sell at a discount in the forward market relative to the spot market.

T F 7. A put option gives the holder the right to sell foreign currency at a specified price and future date.

T F 8. Three-point arbitrage operates to ensure consistent cross exchange rates among currencies.

T F 9. Covered interest arbitrage is another term for speculating that foreign interest rates will rise.

T F10. Destabilizing speculation causes foreign exchange rates to fluctuate more than they otherwise would.

MULTIPLE CHOICE

1. A U.S. importer who must pay 1 million Swiss francs in 90 days can remove the risk of loss from a dollar depreciation by
    a.   purchasing francs in the forward market for 90-day delivery
    b.   selling francs in the forward market for 90-day delivery
    c.   purchasing francs today in the forward market and reselling them in the spot market in 90 days
    d.   selling francs today in the forward market and repurchasing them in the spot market in 90 days

2. The supply schedule for foreign exchange is positively sloped if the foreign demand for a country's currency is
    a.   inelastic
    b.   elastic
    c.   unit elastic (elasticity equal to 1)
    d.   perfectly inelastic (elasticity equal to 0)

3. The real effective exchange rate for the U.S. dollar
    a.   reflects only the influence of merchandise or real trade on the dollar's value
    b.   reflects only activity in the currency futures market
    c.   is the weighted average of the dollar exchange rate relative to the currencies of important U.S. trading partners, adjusted for inflation
    d.   is the weighted average of the dollar exchange rate relative to the currencies of important U.S. trading partners, unadjusted for inflation

4. A decrease in the dollar price of the Japanese yen results in
    a.   Japanese goods becoming less expensive to U.S. residents
    b.   U.S. goods becoming less expensive to Japanese
    c.   Japanese goods becoming less expensive to Japanese
    d.   U.S. goods becoming more expensive to U.S. residents

5. An increase in Canadian demand for Japanese automobiles would cause
    a.   a decrease in supply of Japanese yen to Canada
    b.   an increase in supply of Japanese yen to Canada
    c.   a decrease in Canadian demand for Japanese yen
    d.   an increase in Canadian demand for Japanese yen

6. If inflation were expected to be 8 percent in Britain and 4 percent in Germany over the next year, and the spot exchange rate is 2.5 pounds per euro, one would expect the 180-day forward rate to be approximately
    a.   2.55 pounds per euro
    b.   2.60 pounds per euro
    c.   2.45 pounds per euro
    d.   2.40 pounds per euro

7. If 30-day interest rates were 2 percent in Britain and 8 percent in Germany, covered interest arbitrage would
    a.   influence the forward euro to sell at a discount (fewer pounds per euro than the current spot rate)
    b.   influence the forward euro to sell at a premium (more pounds per euro than the current spot rate)
    c.   provide riskless profits for currency traders
    d.   cause interest rates in Britain and Germany to become equal to each other

113

8.	A difference between forward and futures contracts is that
	a.	forward contracts occur in a specific location
	b.	futures contracts have negotiable delivery dates
	c.	forward contracts can be tailored in amount and delivery date to the needs of importers or exporters
	d.	futures contracts involve no brokerage fees or other transactions costs

9.	Foreign currency options
	a.	give choices or options about which currency to purchase
	b.	commit currency traders to exchange one currency for another
	c.	are used only by hedgers, not by speculators
	d.	provide the right to buy (call) or sell (put) a foreign currency at a specified price within a certain time period

10.	Speculators in foreign exchange markets do all of the following *except*
	a.	attempt to profit by trading on expectations about future currency prices
	b.	bear risk as they attempt to "beat the market"
	c.	attempt to buy currency at a low price and later resell that currency at a higher price
	d.	simultaneously buy a currency at a low price and sell that currency at a higher price, making a riskless profit

PROBLEMS AND SHORT ANSWER QUESTIONS

1.	What is the foreign exchange market? Review your understanding of the different components of the balance-of-payments statement to explain the many different reasons for making foreign exchange market transactions.

2. Consider a U.S.-Japan example and the following graph of supply and demand conditions for the U.S. dollar as a foreign exchange currency. If the current exchange rate is 120 yen per dollar, how would you characterize the U.S. balance-of-payments situation? What is the equilibrium exchange rate? Would the dollar be appreciating or depreciating to reach this rate? Explain how this process would be expected to create an equilibrium balance-of-payments situation.

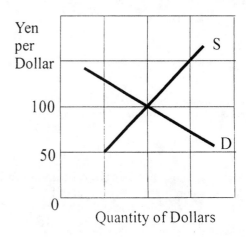

3. In the prior example, explain why the supply curve is shown to be upward-sloping. Under what conditions would this curve instead be downward-sloping? If this were the case, explain why a depreciation of the dollar might not easily restore balance-of-payments equilibrium.

4.   How would a U.S. importer who has agreed to purchase 100 cases of wine in 3 months from a French export firm, payable in euros, use the forward market to hedge against the risk of exchange rate fluctuations over the next 3 months? Would this importer be worried about a dollar appreciation or depreciation?

5.   Suppose that a U.S. construction firm has submitted a yen-denominated bid on a contract in Japan, with the contract bid to be decided in 1 month and the construction to be completed by the successful bidder within 6 months. Explain how and why the firm might use foreign currency options to hedge against currency fluctuations over the next month.

6.   Suppose that the spot exchange rate is 1.6 euros per dollar, and that the *annual* interest rates for 180-day deposits are 4 percent in the United States and 10 percent in Germany. Explain how a U.S. investor would use covered interest arbitrage to hedge against the risk of purchasing a 180-day bill in Germany. Assuming high capital mobility between the United States and Germany, calculate the 180-day forward exchange rate that would be required to eliminate an opportunity for risk-free profits by shifting funds from the United States to Germany.

7.   If current foreign exchange rates were 1.6 euros per dollar, 120 yen per dollar, and 80 yen per euro, explain how a person holding dollars could make a riskless profit by engaging in three point or triangular arbitrage. If the euro/dollar and yen/dollar rates remained unchanged, calculate the yen/euro equilibrium rate to which arbitrage trading would lead.

8.   Explain how not only pure currency traders but also exporters and importers of products and firms engaged in direct foreign investment can engage in foreign exchange rate speculation. What is destabilizing speculation, and why does it pose problems for individuals, for firms, and for national governments?

EXPLORATIONS BEYOND THE CLASSROOM

1.   Consult the financial pages of a recent newspaper such as *The Wall Street Journal* for information on foreign exchange rates and currency cross rates. How do forward rates for British pounds and Japanese yen differ from spot rates? What might be the explanations for these differences?

2.   Consult recent International Monetary Fund publications to find foreign exchange rates that have been relatively stable over the past 5 years, and others that have fluctuated significantly. How stable have been the exchange rates among the dollar, the euro and the yen since 1999?

3.   Locate articles in recent newspapers that deal with foreign exchange rate movements. What explanations do the journalists offer for such fluctuations, and how do these explanations compare with potential causes discussed in the text? If the articles discuss speculation, do they suggest that this foreign currency speculation appears to be stabilizing in nature, or destabilizing?

117

CHAPTER 13

EXCHANGE RATE DETERMINATION

SYNOPSIS OF CHAPTER CONTENT

In the early 1970s the major industrial nations discontinued their policies of supporting their currency exchange rates at fixed or par values. Allowing market forces to determine exchange rates has introduced significant fluctuations in those rates since that time. For instance, the dollar appreciated by nearly 50 percent against the currencies of major U.S. trading partners from 1980 to 1985, and then depreciated by a similar amount in the late 1980s. This chapter explores the theories that have been developed to explain how foreign exchange rates are determined when they are permitted to fluctuate in response to market supply and demand forces.

The **balance-of-payments approach** focuses on the various accounts of the balance-of-payments statement, and shows how changes in any of the categories or components alter equilibrium exchange rates by shifting the foreign exchange supply or demand schedules. As we have seen, the balance of payments reflects the *flow* of funds from one nation to another. Any force that affects debit transactions will shift the demand curve for foreign exchange, while any force that influences credit transactions will shift the supply curve. For instance, in an example involving Britain and the United States, an increase in Britain's income would increase British demand for imports, shifting out the supply curve for pounds and reducing the dollar/pound exchange rate (depreciating the pound). Alternatively, a rise in U.S. income would increase demand for British exports, shifting out the demand curve for pounds and appreciating the pound. Higher inflation in the United States than in Britain would have a similar effect. On the capital account, higher British interest rates also would shift out the demand curve for pounds and cause the pound to appreciate, as would an increased desire by U.S. firms to establish subsidiaries in Britain. Short-term capital movements in response to interest-rate differentials can have significant impacts on exchange rates, as demonstrated in the early 1980s, when high U.S. interest rates contributed to a major dollar appreciation. Such capital flows occur, however, only if the higher interest rates are not expected to be offset by currency depreciation caused by inflation; in general it is **real** (inflation-adjusted) rather than **nominal** interest-rate differentials that generate international capital flows and influence exchange rates. In practice, it is difficult to use the balance-of-payments approach to predict exchange rate movements, partly because it reflects longer-term forces rather than factors that cause short-term volatility, and also because developments affecting one component of the balance-of-payments accounts may push the exchange rate in the opposite direction from factors affecting another component.

A more specific method of predicting exchange rate movements is the **purchasing-power parity-approach**. The fundamental basis for this approach is the **law of one price**, which contends that exchange rates will adjust so that the price of any single good will be the same in all nations, abstracting from transportation costs and trade barriers. Generalizing from this, the price of similar market baskets of goods should be identical in all nations, and from this, the **relative** purchasing-power-parity approach predicts that the foreign exchange rate of a currency initially in equilibrium will adjust to reflect differences between domestic and foreign inflation. Thus, a country experiencing higher inflation than its trading partners would find its currency depreciating by a corresponding amount. By focusing on inflation differentials, this theory implicitly assumes that only trade in goods and services influences exchange rates, thus ignoring the often significant impact of capital flows on exchange rates. Furthermore, by utilizing broad indicators such as the consumer price index as measures of inflation, it fails to recognize that prices of only those goods that are tradeable may not follow such patterns perfectly. Finally, the theory does not capture the potential impact of government trade restrictions on exchange rates. Over longer periods of time and for pairs of countries without significant capital flows between them, the purchasing-power-parity approach performs relatively well. However, it is of much less value to those attempting to predict short-run exchange rate movements.

A number of economists who find shortcomings in the balance-of-payments approach and its variants that focus on the *flow* of funds to predict exchange rates have developed as an alternative the **monetary approach**, which views changes in the *stocks* of national currencies as determinants of exchange rates. This approach views the balance of payments as a monetary phenomenon, whereby increases or decreases in a nation's domestic money supply or demand cause that nation's currency to rise or fall in value relative to other currencies. For example, an increase in the U.S. money supply creates an initial excess supply of money in the United States, and also facilitates an increase in U.S. income and a reduction in U.S. interest rates. These developments will increase the U.S. demand for foreign exchange, depreciating the dollar and increasing domestic prices. All of this operates to increase transactions demand for dollars in the United States, eliminating the excess supply of money. Essentially, the monetary approach views a depreciation as resulting from an excess supply of a nation's stock of monetary assets. Correspondingly, increased demand for money unaccompanied by an increase in the nation's stock or supply of money would cause that nation's currency to appreciate in value relative to other currencies. Although this approach brings attention to the often-neglected importance of monetary variables in exchange rate determination, empirical support is mixed and the monetary approach is not viewed by most economists as a fully adequate substitute for more traditional approaches.

An extension of the monetary approach to exchange rate determination is the **asset-markets** or **portfolio-balance approach**. This approach recognizes that international capital movements have both continuing-flow and stock-adjustment components, but like the monetary approach it emphasizes the stock-adjustment dimension. The reason for this is that financial and nonfinancial corporations today have such large portfolios of domestic and foreign financial assets that adjustments in the mix of assets in those portfolios can have balance-of-payments impacts that dwarf the influence of normal capital account investment flows. The asset-markets approach maintains that higher interest rates on financial assets denominated in one nation's currency relative to interest rates on assets in another currency will induce investors to alter their portfolios to include more assets in the higher interest rate currency. The process of adjusting to achieve the new desired portfolio will involve international capital flows captured on the capital account of the balance of payments. Sudden changes in investor expectations about risk or return associated with specific financial assets, or sudden changes in government or corporate supply of such assets, would cause those investors to alter their desired global portfolios of financial assets, and the international capital flows required to achieve such portfolios would cause significant exchange rate movements. Empirical support for the asset-markets approach has been mixed, but it may well help to explain the short-term volatility of exchange rates among major currencies in recent decades.

Thus, exchange rate fluctuations can be caused by changing expectations about either private market conditions or government monetary and fiscal policies. Another factor that contributes to exchange rate volatility is the phenomenon of **overshooting**. Exchange rates adjust to equate supply and demand for a nation's currency. Because short-term elasticities of demand for exports and imports are lower than longer-term elasticities, the magnitude of a depreciation required to eliminate a balance-of-payments deficit will be greater in the short run than in the long run. Also, the fact that domestic prices tend to be stickier or less flexible in the short run than are exchange rates causes exchange rates to move further than otherwise would be necessary in response to changing supply or demand conditions. For both of these reasons, exchange rates tend to move beyond or overshoot their new long-term equilibrium in immediate response to market disturbances, eventually recovering or returning partially as elasticities increase and domestic prices adjust.

A number of consulting firms and other groups and individuals regularly forecast exchange rate movements for their clients. Some use **fundamental analysis**, basing their forecasts on econometric models of the global economy's fundamental economic structure. Such forecasts often also incorporate subjective assessments of economic conditions, and other analysts who rely more exclusively on such subjective evaluations produce what are called **judgmental forecasts** of exchange rates. Finally, another group of forecasters bases predictions on **technical analysis**, simply looking for recurring patterns in economic and financial data and predicting particular exchange rate movements whenever certain patterns emerge. Although in this chapter we have identified several approaches to exchange-rate determination that offer useful insights, the fact that no single method has been found to be wholly adequate is reflected also in the rather discouraging record of consulting firms, whose forecasts of future spot exchange rates rarely are more accurate than the publicly available forward exchange rates.

KEY CONCEPTS AND TERMS (Define each concept, and briefly explain its significance.)

Balance-of-payments approach to exchange-rate determination

International capital flows

Nominal versus real interest-rate differentials

Purchasing-power-parity approach

Law of one price

Monetary approach

Asset-markets approach

Exchange-rate overshooting

Fundamental, judgmental, and technical forecasting

TRUE OR FALSE? (On an exam, be prepared to explain *why* the statement is true or false.)

T F 1.   More rapid economic growth in the United States than in Britain would cause the dollar to appreciate relative to the pound.

T F 2. Higher inflation in the United States than in Britain would cause the dollar to depreciate relative to the pound.

T F 3. Higher real interest rates in Britain than in the United States would cause the dollar to appreciate relative to the pound.

T F 4. The law of one price demonstrates that tariffs cannot affect prices of imported products.

T F 5. The monetary approach to exchange-rate determination deals with flow rather than stock concepts.

T F 6. Market expectations of higher returns on dollar-denominated assets would cause the dollar to appreciate in value.

T F 7. Low demand elasticities contribute to short-term exchange rate volatility and overshooting.

T F 8. Fundamental analysis is another name for the use of technical analysis to forecast exchange rates.

T F 9. Fundamental analysis uses econometric models of the global economy to predict exchange rate movements.

T F10. Consulting firms generally have been quite successful at forecasting short-term exchange rate fluctuations.

MULTIPLE CHOICE

1. According to the balance-of-payments approach, rapid economic growth in the United States compared to that in Europe and Japan would lead to
   a. larger U.S. trade deficits and an appreciating dollar
   b. smaller U.S. trade deficits and an appreciating dollar
   c. larger U.S. trade deficits and a depreciating dollar
   d. smaller U.S. trade deficits and a depreciating dollar

2. If nominal interest rates rose by 3 percentage points and inflationary expectations rose by 5 percentage points in the United States,
   a. capital would be expected to flow into the United States
   b. the dollar would be expected to depreciate
   c. the dollar would be expected to appreciate
   d. the dollar would remain stable relative to other currencies

3. The relative purchasing-power-parity theory would predict that if inflation is 10 percent in Britain and 4 percent in the United States,
   a. the dollar would appreciate by 4 percent against the pound
   b. the dollar would depreciate by 4 percent against the pound
   c. the dollar would appreciate by 6 percent against the pound
   d. the dollar would depreciate by 6 percent against the pound

4. The purchasing-power-parity theory has shortcomings in predicting exchange rate movements for all of the following reasons *except*
    a. not all products are internationally tradeable
    b. governments sometimes restrict exports and imports
    c. international capital flows affect exchange rates
    d. inflation affects exchange rates

5. According to the monetary approach to exchange rate determination, a nation's payments deficit is the result of
    a. domestic interest rates being higher than rates abroad
    b. domestic interest rates being lower than rates abroad
    c. the domestic demand for money exceeding the supply of money
    d. the domestic supply of money exceeding the demand for money

6. The asset-markets approach views exchange rates as being determined primarily by
    a. relative growth rates of GDP between countries
    b. the merchandise trade balance of each country
    c. efforts of investors to balance their portfolios among financial assets denominated in different currencies
    d. the use of import tariffs and quotas by governments

7. According to the asset-markets approach, increased investor confidence in the Mexican economy would cause the peso to
    a. appreciate because of an increased supply of peso-denominated assets
    b. depreciate because of an increased supply of peso-denominated assets
    c. appreciate because of an increased demand for peso-denominated assets
    d. depreciate because of an increased demand for peso-denominated assets

8. The asset-markets approach is most helpful in explaining
    a. why exchange rates remain quite stable
    b. why governments change their money supplies
    c. long-term exchange rate movements
    d. short-term exchange rate volatility

9. Exchange rate overshooting often occurs
    a. because domestic prices adjust quickly to demand shifts
    b. because of military spending during global conflicts
    c. because export demand is inelastic in the short run
    d. because export demand is elastic in the short run

10. Consulting firms that use large-scale econometric models to forecast exchange rate movements
    a. are engaging in judgmental forecasts
    b. are engaging in fundamental analysis
    c. are engaging in technical analysis
    d. use the forward rate to predict spot exchange rate movements

PROBLEMS AND SHORT ANSWER QUESTIONS

1.   From 1980 to 1985, the United States had persistent trade deficits, but also significant capital inflows because of high interest rates relative to those in other industrial nations. Use the balance-of-payments approach to exchange-rate determination to explain the impact of each of these two factors on the value of the dollar relative to other currencies. Since the dollar appreciated significantly during this time period, which balance-of-payments account must have had the most important impact on the exchange rate? How would this dollar appreciation have affected the U.S. trade balance?

2.   Use the purchasing-power-parity theory to predict the impact on the dollar/peso exchange rate if Mexico experiences 40 percent inflation during the coming year while the United States experiences 4 percent inflation. What are the most important limitations of this theory? Why might it be a better predictor of the dollar/peso exchange rates over the long run than of the exchange rate between the dollar and (a) the Japanese yen or (b) the Russian ruble?

3.   Why are capital flows said to depend on real rather than nominal interest-rate differentials between countries? If nominal short-term interest rates were 8 percent in the United States and 6 percent in Canada, with inflation rates of 4 percent in the United States and 1 per cent in Canada, explain in which direction short-term capital would flow and whether the U.S. dollar would appreciate or depreciate relative to the Canadian dollar. How would your answer regarding international capital flows be different if the U.S. and Canadian governments committed themselves to maintaining fixed exchange rates between their two currencies?

123

4.   Why is the monetary approach to exchange-rate determination said to be a stock-adjustment rather than a flow approach? How would an increase in the U.S. money supply relative to the Canadian money supply be expected to affect the exchange rate between the U.S. and Canadian dollars?

5.   Explain how the asset-markets approach can be considered a more comprehensive version of the monetary approach to exchange-rate determination. Using this approach, explain how it might be possible for the U.S. dollar to appreciate relative to the yen even if the U.S. money supply were increasing more rapidly than the Japanese money supply.

6.   How does the phenomenon of overshooting contribute to short-term exchange-rate volatility? What policies might governments adopt if they wished to either reduce or control such volatility, short of adopting fixed exchange rates?

7.   Contrast judgmental forecasts, fundamental analysis, and technical analysis as alternative methods for predicting exchange-rate movements. How successful have such methods been? Why do even those consultants who utilize fundamental analysis also incorporate subjective judgments in making exchange-rate forecasts?

EXPLORATIONS BEYOND THE CLASSROOM

1.   Consult a recent issue of the International Monetary Fund's *International Financial Statistics*, and select for examination two countries with quite different inflation experiences over the past 10 years. Use the data for inflation rates and exchange-rate movements for these countries to determine how closely the results match the predictions of the purchasing-power parity theory. How accurate is the theory over periods as short as 1 year? How accurate is it for the full 10-year period?

2.   Review recent newspaper reports of exchange-rate fluctuations among major currencies. What evidence do you find of balance-of-payments approaches being used to explain the observed fluctuations? To what extent is there a focus on monetary policy in explaining currency appreciations or depreciations? Do you find aspects of the broader asset-markets approach present in the analysis?

3.   Examine recent newsletters or international financial reports of a major bank such as Chase Manhattan, Chemical Bank, or Citibank for exchange-rate or currency forecasts. What is the primary forecasting method being utilized? Can you find evidence that the bank is drawing on more than one basic method in supporting its exchange-rate forecasts?

CHAPTER 14

BALANCE-OF-PAYMENTS ADJUSTMENTS
UNDER FIXED EXCHANGE RATES

SYNOPSIS OF CHAPTER CONTENT

We saw in Chapter 11 that in one sense the balance of payments always balances, because the double-entry accounting system ensures that credits and debits are equal and that the balance is zero when all transactions are included. However, a nation may well have a cumulative deficit on current and capital accounts, reflecting a trade deficit and capital outflows, which it is financing by drawing down its international reserve assets. Once these reserves are depleted, other methods of adjustment to eliminate the current and capital account deficits must be found. Similarly, although nations with persistent current and capital account surpluses may choose simply to increase their reserve holdings, even they may decide that adjustments to achieve trade balance would be preferable to continuing to acquire reserve assets and investments in other countries. This chapter focuses on adjustment methods for eliminating balance-of-payments deficits or surpluses under conditions of fixed exchange rates.

The classical **gold standard** for balance-of-payments adjustment existed from the late 1800s to the early 1900s, and emerged from David Hume's earlier analysis of the self-defeating nature of mercantilist trade policies. Adherence to the gold standard required nations to back their domestic money supplies with gold reserves, and consequently to increase or decrease their money supplies proportionately as their gold reserves rose or fell. The classical economists also accepted the **quantity theory of money**, reflected in the equation of exchange that $MV = PQ$ and the classical belief that monetary velocity (V) would be constant and that real output (Q) would be fixed at full employment, so that a change in the money supply (M) would simply affect the domestic price level (P). Thus, gold standard adherents believed that a nation with a trade deficit would finance that deficit with gold reserves, reduce its money supply as its gold reserves fell, and then experience a corresponding reduction in domestic prices. A nation with a trade surplus would acquire additional gold reserves, increase its money supply, and experience higher domestic prices. These lower prices in the deficit nation would increase its exports and reduce its imports, while higher prices in the surplus nation would operate to make its exports less competitive and imports more attractive. Thus, the workings of the gold standard would automatically correct trade imbalances among countries and achieve balance-of-payments equilibrium.

Interest-rate adjustments also would be expected to reinforce the workings of the gold standard in achieving automatic balance-of-payments equilibrium. A nation losing gold and decreasing its money supply because of a trade deficit also would experience rising interest rates as credit became less available, while expansionary monetary policy in the surplus nation would bring falling interest rates there. The resulting interest-rate differential would encourage capital to flow from the surplus to the deficit nation, creating a capital account surplus to offset the trade deficit of the first nation. Although this would more quickly restore balance-of-payments equilibrium than if only current account adjustments occurred, such capital flows might be temporary, as trade surplus nations showed unwillingness to finance the deficits of other nations with ongoing capital flows.

Critics of the gold standard noted that its assumption of perfect domestic price flexibility often was unrealistic. Reduction in a nation's money supply might well reduce Q rather than P, causing recession and unemployment rather than falling prices. Surplus nations might also wish to avoid the inflationary consequences of an increased money supply. Additional complications arise if V is not stable or predictable. Thus, central banks often refused to play by the rules of the game, and refused to increase or decrease their money supplies in response to gains or losses of gold reserves.

Skeptics of the gold standard emphasized that **income adjustments** more likely would be required to restore balance-of-payments equilibrium for deficit nations under conditions of fixed exchange rates. This analysis grew out of the **income determination** theory developed by John Maynard Keynes in the

1930s to explain the persistence of unemployment during the Great Depression. In a closed economy without trade, income determination models showed that total spending in an economy (Y) would consist of consumer expenditures (C) plus business investment spending (I), and that total national income (also equal to Y) would consist of consumption (C) plus saving (S). Thus, in equilibrium, C + I would equal total output (Y), and saving would also equal investment (S = I, or S – I = 0). Keynes also hypothesized that individuals have a marginal propensity to consume a certain fraction (c) of additional income, and thus a marginal propensity to save the remaining fraction (s = 1 – c). This means that an increase in investment spending will have a multiplied impact on the economy as individuals engage in additional rounds of spending in response to the increased income earned by producing the investment goods. The ultimate increase in income will equal 1/(1 – c) or 1/s times the initial increase in investment.

These principles remain the same in an open economy with exports and imports, but the results differ in some important ways. Exports (X) must be added as a component of total expenditures or GDP, and imports (M) must be subtracted from consumption and investment spending so as not to include in GDP any spending on goods and services produced in other countries. This means that now S = I + X – M, or S + M = I + X. This is another way of recognizing that total leakages out of the circular flow system or money not spent on domestic goods must equal the injections of additional demand into the system in the form of investment and export spending. Alternatively, this can be stated as S – I = X – M, indicating that an excess of domestic saving over investment is matched by a trade surplus, or that a trade deficit will mean that domestic saving is too small to completely finance investment spending. Another dimension of the open economy is to recognize that imports depend on income (M = mY) just as consumption spending does. A consequence of this is that, because imports constitute a leakage of spending outside the domestic economy, the multiplier effect will be smaller than before, 1/(s + m) rather than simply 1/s.

Several important consequences flow from this open economy model of income determination. First, the smaller multiplier resulting from the import leakages means that an increase in investment spending will generate a smaller increase in GDP than in the simpler closed economy context. Second, changes in GDP resulting from increased investment spending or exports also will have balance-of-payments impacts because imports vary with income. For instance, the multiplier effects of increased investment spending will reduce a nation's trade surplus or increase its trade deficit as imports rise with income. An export-led expansion would have the same effect on GDP, but the initial increase in trade surplus resulting from higher exports would be reduced as the higher income brought with it more spending on imports. Perhaps of greatest consequence, in a world of fixed exchange rates and inflexible domestic prices, this income adjustment model indicates that the only way for a nation to reduce its trade deficit is to reduce its income or GDP in order to reduce imports. This is a more direct recognition of the fear expressed by critics of the gold standard, that resolving a trade deficit in a world of fixed exchange rates might bring serious unemployment and recession rather than falling domestic prices.

Foreign repercussions of domestic income changes may also be important in some situations. If a major trading nation experiences income growth arising from a boost to investment, its increased imports resulting from this growth also represent increased income for its trading partners, and they in turn will increase their imports from the first nation, raising that nation's exports and reinforcing its income growth. The same process would work in reverse, of course, with a nation going into economic recession transmitting adverse effects to its trading partners by reducing its imports, and later experiencing further negative feedback effects as those nations respond to falling income by reducing their imports.

Finally, the **monetary approach**, discussed in earlier chapters, provides an alternative view of automatic adjustment to balance-of-payments deficits. This approach maintains that a balance-of-payments deficit is simply the result of an excess supply of monetary assets over the demand for such monetary assets in the home country. As a country finances its trade deficits by giving up international reserves, it will reduce its money supply, eliminating the excess supply of monetary assets and automatically restoring balance-of-payments equilibrium without either exchange-rate movements or income adjustments. Although the monetary approach provides important insights regarding the importance of monetary variables in causing trade deficits, its view of the adjustment process very closely parallels that of the gold standard and thus is subject to the same limitations. In particular, a money supply reduction in response to a trade deficit may correct the deficit only by causing a reduction in domestic income and employment, rather than through a smooth, automatic process of asset and price adjustments.

KEY CONCEPTS AND TERMS (Define each concept, and briefly explain its significance.)

Gold standard

Quantity theory of money

Monetary and price adjustments

Rules of the game (gold standard)

Interest rate adjustments and international capital flows

Keynesian income determination model

Closed economy multiplier

Foreign trade multiplier

Income adjustments to achieve balance-of-payments equilibrium

Foreign repercussion effect

TRUE OR FALSE? (On an exam, be prepared to explain *why* the statement is true or false.)

T F 1.   The gold standard depended on exchange-rate flexibility to correct balance-of-payments deficits.

T F 2.   Under the gold standard, a country with a balance-of-payments deficit would be expected to reduce its money supply and experience domestic price level reductions.

T F 3.   The classical quantity theory of money supporters held that velocity would be stable and that income would remain at full employment.

T F 4.   Under the gold standard, higher interest rates and capital inflows would be expected to contribute to automatic adjustment for a country with a balance-of-payments deficit.

T F 5.   Fear of domestic unemployment led governments to resist the rules of the game under the gold standard.

T F 6.   The foreign trade multiplier in an open economy is larger than the simple multiplier of a closed domestic economy.

T F 7.   In the income determination model, an increase in a nation's income would contribute to a rising trade surplus.

T F 8.   The income adjustment model indicates that a nation might be required to reduce its GDP in order to correct a trade deficit.

T F 9.   The foreign repercussion effect of the income determination model predicts that foreign nations will retaliate against trade deficits by raising import tariffs.

T F10.   The monetary approach maintains that the fundamental cause of a balance-of-payments deficit is a domestic money supply that exceeds domestic demand for money.

MULTIPLE CHOICE

1.   Under the historic gold standard, a nation with a balance-of-payments surplus would acquire reserves and would experience
   a.   an appreciating exchange rate
   b.   a depreciating exchange rate
   c.   an increased money supply, rising prices, and a diminishing surplus
   d.   an increased money supply, falling prices, and a growing surplus

2.   Under the historic gold standard, if Great Britain realized a payments deficit that led to a gold outflow and a decrease in the money supply, Britain would experience a
   a.   fall in interest rates and short-term capital inflows
   b.   fall in interest rates and short-term capital outflows
   c.   rise in interest rates and short-term capital inflows
   d.   rise in interest rates and short-term capital outflows

3. According to the quantity theory of money, a 10 percent increase in the domestic money supply will result in
   a. a 10 percent increase in the domestic price level
   b. a more than 10 percent increase in the domestic price level
   c. a 10 percent decrease in the domestic price level
   d. a more than 10 percent decrease in the domestic price level

4. Government authorities in nations with balance-of-payments deficits declined to play by the rules of the gold standard
   a. because they feared inflation
   b. because they did not have any international reserves
   c. in order to prevent exchange rates from fluctuating
   d. to avoid potential recession and high unemployment

5. A likely consequence of economic recession and falling sales and profits in Canada would be
   a. increasing foreign investment in securities issued by the Canadian government
   b. decreasing foreign investment in securities issued by the Canadian government
   c. increasing direct private foreign investment in Canada
   d. decreasing direct private foreign investment in Canada

6. If investment increased by $100 in a nation with a marginal propensity to consume of 0.8 and a marginal propensity to import of 0.05,
   a. income would rise by $500 and imports would rise by $25
   b. income would rise by $100 and imports would rise by $5
   c. income would rise by $400 and imports would rise by $20
   d. income would rise by $400 and the trade deficit would decrease by $20

7. The income adjustment approach would require a nation with a trade deficit of $100 and a marginal propensity to import of 0.05 to
   a. reduce its income by $2,000
   b. reduce its income by $500
   c. increase its income by $2,000
   d. increase its income by $500

8. Open economy equilibrium income determination requires that
   a. saving equal investment
   b. exports equal imports
   c. saving minus investment equal exports minus imports
   d. investment minus saving equal exports minus imports

9. The foreign repercussion effect for a nation with an investment boom, a rising GDP, and a growing trade deficit
   a. would be important only if the nation were small
   b. is caused by tariff retaliation among trading partners
   c. would make the trade deficit even larger
   d. would make the trade deficit somewhat smaller

10. According to the monetary approach to the balance of payments, a nation's payments deficit is the result of
   a. domestic interest rates being higher than rates abroad
   b. domestic interest rates being lower than rates abroad
   c. domestic demand for money exceeding the supply of money
   d. the supply of money exceeding domestic demand for money

PROBLEMS AND SHORT ANSWER QUESTIONS

1.   Suppose that the United States experienced a balance-of-payments deficit under the gold standard with fixed exchange rates. Explain each step in the envisioned automatic adjustment process to eliminate the deficit. Why might the U.S. government refrain from following the rules of the game?

2.   Explain how interest-rate adjustments and international capital flows would reinforce the adjustment process under the gold standard. How would this process become more complicated if investors were not confident that exchange rates would remain fixed?

3. Consider an economy in which people spend $50 plus 80 percent of their income on consumer goods, business spends $200 on investment, foreigners purchase $100 of exports, and residents spend 5 percent of their income on imports.

    a. Determine equilibrium income for this economy. Determine the levels of saving and of imports, and explain whether the equilibrium condition relating to saving, imports, investment, and exports is met in this economy.

    b. Draw the (S – I) and (X – M) curves below to verify graphically your results for part a. Why is this equivalent to showing that (S + M) equals (I + X)?

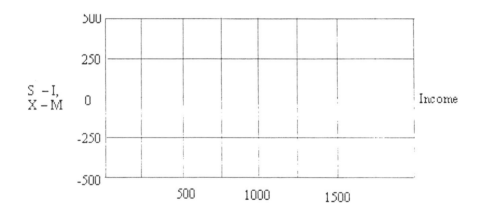

c. Now assume that increased business optimism raises planned investment spending to $300. What is the foreign trade multiplier for this economy? Use this to determine the new level of equilibrium income. What will happen to the trade balance? Does $(S - I)$ still equal $(X - M)$? Explain.

d. Show the effects of this investment spending increase on your graph for part b. How does the graph show the impact on income and on the trade balance?

e. Compare the effects on income and on the trade balance if export demand rather than investment spending had increased by $100.

4. Suppose that the U.S. economy began to grow rapidly because of increased business investment spending. Why would the resulting multiplier effects be smaller than if the United States were in a closed economy with no trade? Explain how the foreign repercussion effects of this expansion would affect GDP and the trade balance in the United States.

5. Explain how the monetary approach would view the automatic elimination of a balance-of-payments deficit in a fixed exchange-rate world. How might our earlier experience with the gold standard suggest that the envisioned adjustment process of the monetary approach may not be so smooth and automatic?

EXPLORATIONS BEYOND THE CLASSROOM

1. Consult recent newspapers for articles dealing with efforts of national governments to stabilize or fix the exchange rates of their currencies relative to other currencies. What evidence do you find that these governments are undertaking income adjustments, interest-rate adjustments, or monetary adjustments in order to resolve balance-of-payments problems while maintaining stable exchange rates?

2. Locate articles dealing with balance-of-payments issues involving the EC countries, the United States, and Japan. What evidence do you find that foreign repercussion effects are influencing the policy recommendations made by government leaders in these nations?

3. Consult newspapers or magazines published in Europe for discussions of internal balance-of-payments conflicts among EC members. Given the commitment to fixed exchange rates among EC members, and the recent adoption of the euro as a single currency among some EC members, how do your articles reflect the dilemmas of balance-of-payments adjustment under fixed exchange rates?

134

CHAPTER 15

EXCHANGE RATE ADJUSTMENTS AND
THE BALANCE OF PAYMENTS

SYNOPSIS OF CHAPTER CONTENT

We have seen in previous chapters that countries operating under conditions of fixed exchange rates often face difficult choices in dealing with balance-of-payments deficits. The automatic adjustment mechanisms envisioned by advocates of the gold standard often do not work smoothly, and nations that use restrictive monetary or fiscal policies to eliminate deficits find that domestic recession and unemployment, rather than falling prices, may be the consequence. This chapter focuses on an alternative approach, analyzing how exchange rate adjustments may be used to restore balance-of-payments equilibrium.

Within a fixed exchange rate system, a government may exercise the option to **devalue** its currency, reducing its exchange value relative to gold or to other reserve assets. Such a formal devaluation also would cause the currency to **depreciate** or to lose value relative to other national currencies, unless of course these currencies were devalued to the same extent by their governments. Alternatively, a government may choose to **revalue** its currency, raising its exchange value, in which case the currency also normally would **appreciate** or rise in value relative to other national currencies. What we must explore is how such exchange rate adjustments are likely to affect a nation's balance of payments.

Suppose that the U.S. dollar appreciates relative to the German mark. A steel producer in the United States that relies exclusively upon domestic inputs will not have its dollar costs affected, but because of the dollar appreciation the mark cost of steel exports from the United States will have risen, and U.S. steel will become less competitive in world markets. Essentially, a 10 percent appreciation of the dollar would make U.S. steel exports 10 percent more expensive from the vantage point of German importers paying marks. This effect would be moderated to the extent that steel produced in the United States utilized some inputs from other countries such as Germany. The appreciated dollar would lower the dollar cost of mark-denominated imported inputs from Germany, thus reducing the dollar cost of steel and enabling U.S. firms to reduce their dollar prices of exports. The net result would be that the price increase of U.S. steel exports in the importing nations such as Germany would be less than if all inputs came from within the United States. Given the increasing internationalization of production, with components of individual products coming from many different nations, this modification is potentially quite significant. Firms also may respond to a currency appreciation by reducing their profit margins in order to preserve a competitive position in export markets. For all of these reasons, export and import prices may be slow to adjust to exchange rate movements and may change by only a fraction of the appreciation or depreciation.

If a country wishes to improve its competitiveness in export markets and reduce a trade deficit by devaluing its currency, what conditions must be met for this to be a successful strategy? The **elasticity approach** focuses on how responsive purchasers in each country are to changes in relative prices of exports and imports. As noted earlier, *elasticity of demand* measures responsiveness of buyers to price changes. More specifically, demand is said to be *elastic* if quantity demanded changes more in percentage terms than does the price (again in percentage terms) that brings about that change in quantity demanded. Demand is *unitary elastic* if price and quantity changes are equal in percentage terms, and *inelastic* if quantity demanded changes by less in percentage terms than the associated price change. Stated in numerical terms, demand is elastic if this ratio of demand and price percentage changes is greater than 1, and inelastic if it is less than 1.

Consider the effects of a U.S. dollar devaluation designed to reduce a U.S. trade deficit. The devaluation will make U.S. exports less expensive in other countries, and if the dollar prices of exports do not change these nations will increase their total demand for dollars to pay for U.S. exports; the larger their demand elasticity, the greater will be their increased demand for dollars. Similarly, if U.S. demand for imports is elastic, people in the United States will significantly reduce their purchases of imports as their prices rise, and spend fewer total dollars on such imports. However, if U.S. demand for imports is inelastic, the quantity demanded will decline in percentage terms by less than the import prices rise in percentage terms, and U.S. residents will spend more rather than fewer dollars on such imports. In fact, if both U.S. and foreign demand are inelastic, a dollar devaluation would actually increase the U.S. trade deficit rather than diminish it, because the increased dollars flowing out of the United States in payment for U.S. imports would exceed any increased foreign demand for dollars to pay for U.S. exports. Thus, conditions for a devaluation to successfully reduce a deficit are summarized in what is known as the **Marshall-Lerner condition**, which states that a devaluation or depreciation will improve the nation's trade balance only if the sum of the importing nation's demand for imports and the foreign demand for that nation's exports is greater than 1. Although there was considerable *elasticity pessimism* during the 1940s and 1950s, since the 1960s most economists have been *elasticity optimists*, and empirical studies support such optimism with their estimates that the sum of import and export demand elasticities is well above 1 for most nations.

Despite such optimism, analysts have observed that devaluations may take some time to be successful; the time path of adjustment follows what is known as the **J-curve effect**, with a devaluing nation's trade balance initially declining or growing worse before it eventually reverses its decline and begins to improve. In essence, a series of lags delays the demand responses to price changes; such lags relate to recognition delays, time for decision making, delays in placing new orders until existing inventories are depleted, time required to increase production once new orders are placed, and time required for ultimate delivery. What this means is that short-term demand elasticities appear to be quite low, and only after 2 or more years have these elasticities risen to levels that bring improved trade balances after a devaluation.

Another factor that may limit or delay the effectiveness of a devaluation is the phenomenon of the **currency pass-through relationship**. As indicated earlier, export firms may reduce their domestic currency prices and reduce their profit margins after a revaluation in order to limit the extent of price increases in foreign currencies and thereby preserve their market positions; and import-competing firms in the devaluing nation may take advantage of their improved positions by increasing their domestic prices and their profit margins rather than simply increasing sales. Thus, there may be only a partial pass-through of the price realignments expected from a devaluation, thereby limiting its potential beneficial effect on the trade balance.

Even when elasticity conditions are favorable for a successful devaluation, the **absorption approach** identifies additional conditions that must be met in order for an improved trade balance to become a reality. This approach draws on the basic macroeconomic identity relating total domestic output (Y) to the demand components of consumption (C), domestic investment (I), government spending (G), and net exports (X – M), or

$$Y = C + I + G + (X - M)$$

The first three components represent domestic absorption of or demand for goods and services (A), and the final term represents the trade balance (B). Thus, the equation above can be written as

$$Y = A + B$$

The policy implication of this identity is that a devaluation that offers the potential for improving the trade balance (B) can succeed only if Y also increases or A is reduced. If an economy is operating well below full employment, the excess capacity is available for increasing net export production and increasing Y. However, an economy operating at or near full employment would be required to take restrictive monetary or fiscal measures to reduce domestic absorption (A) in order to release productive resources for improving its trade balance (B). Without such "belt-tightening" measures of restraint, a

136

devaluation under such circumstances would simply generate excess demand and inflation, which in turn would negate or nullify the intended price improvements from a devaluation. The absorption approach recognizes that improving a nation's trade balance may require fundamental adjustments within the domestic economy, not simply changes in the foreign trade sector.

Finally, the **monetary approach** recognizes that a balance-of-payments deficit must be viewed as involving not only the current account or the trade balance but also the capital account. By increasing domestic import prices and perhaps domestic income, a devaluation will increase the demand for money, which will attract an inflow of money from abroad if the domestic money supply is not increased. Such inflow creates a temporary surplus, which will be reduced once domestic absorption increases, and over the long run a devaluation will only raise domestic prices and not reduce the trade deficit. This approach essentially views a balance-of-payments deficit as a monetary phenomenon, and has in common with the absorption approach an emphasis on the need for fundamental domestic policy adjustments in order to restore trade balance.

KEY CONCEPTS AND TERMS (Define each concept, and briefly explain its significance.)

Devaluation

Depreciation

Revaluation

Appreciation

Elasticity approach to exchange rate adjustment

Marshall-Lerner condition

J-curve effect

Currency pass-through

137

Absorption approach to exchange rate adjustment

Monetary approach to exchange rate adjustment

TRUE OR FALSE? (On an exam, be prepared to explain *why* the statement is true or false.)

T F 1. A devaluation is a government decision to lower the exchange value of its currency.

T F 2. An appreciation is a fall in the value of one currency relative to other national currencies.

T F 3. Currency depreciations but not devaluations are possible within a floating exchange rate system.

T F 4. A devaluation is most successful in eliminating a trade deficit when export and import demand elasticities are very low.

T F 5. Firms in a nation whose currency appreciates will experience a smaller loss in global competitiveness to the extent that they utilize imported inputs in production.

T F 6. The J-curve effect indicates that a devaluation is likely to increase a trade deficit initially, and only after a period of 2 to 4 years bring significant deficit reduction.

T F 7. Currency pass-through measures the extent to which governments allow tourists to bring foreign currencies into their countries.

T F 8. The absorption approach predicts that a devaluation will be most successful in a nation operating at full employment.

T F 9. If a nation is operating at full employment, a restrictive fiscal policy may also be required for a devaluation to improve the nation's trade balance.

T F10. The monetary approach predicts that a devaluation will reduce a nation's trade deficit only if the government also increases its money supply at the time of the devaluation.

MULTIPLE CHOICE

1. Suppose that in a fixed exchange rate world the United States changes the value of the dollar from 100 yen to 80 yen and Britain changes the value of the pound from 150 yen to 120 yen. This would mean that the dollar has
   a. appreciated against the yen but not the pound
   b. appreciated against the yen and the pound
   c. depreciated against the yen but not the pound
   d. depreciated against the yen and the pound

2. If Microsoft obtains all of its inputs in the United States and these costs are denominated in dollars, an appreciation of the dollar's exchange value
   a. adds to the firm's international competitiveness
   b. detracts from the firm's international competitiveness
   c. does not affect the firm's international competitiveness
   d. either adds to or subtracts from the firm's international competitiveness, depending on demand elasticity

3. If Boeing obtains jet engines from the United Kingdom and the price of these engines is denominated in pounds, an appreciation of the dollar will lead to a _____ in the pound cost of an aircraft produced by Boeing and a _____ in the dollar cost of that aircraft, compared with the cost changes that would occur if all inputs for aircraft production came from the United States and were dollar-denominated.
   a. smaller increase, smaller decrease
   b. smaller increase, larger decrease
   c. larger increase, smaller decrease
   d. larger increase, larger decrease

4. If U.S. demand for imports is inelastic, a devaluation of the dollar will
   a. significantly reduce the outflow of dollars paid for imports
   b. slightly reduce the outflow of dollars paid for imports
   c. increase the outflow of dollars paid for imports
   d. leave unchanged the outflow of dollars paid for imports

5. According to the Marshall-Lerner condition, currency depreciation results in an improvement in Britain's trade balance when the
   a. British demand for imports is elastic and the foreign demand for British exports is elastic
   b. British demand for imports is elastic and the foreign demand for British exports is inelastic
   c. British demand for imports is inelastic and the foreign demand for British exports is elastic
   d. British demand for imports is inelastic and the foreign demand for British exports is inelastic

6. If European companies slash profit margins and reduce manufacturing costs in response to a depreciation of the dollar's exchange value, this will
   a. lengthen the time required for the depreciation to reduce a U.S. trade surplus
   b. lengthen the time required for the depreciation to reduce a U.S. trade deficit
   c. shorten the time required for the depreciation to reduce a U.S. trade surplus
   d. shorten the time required for the depreciation to reduce a U.S. trade deficit

7. The J-curve effect is likely to be more pronounced to the extent that
   a. new suppliers are difficult to locate and evaluate
   b. short-term supply and demand elasticities are high
   c. parts inventories of imported components are low
   d. firms can quickly adjust production to increases in orders

8. According to the absorption approach, the economic circumstance that best justifies currency devaluation is when the home country experiences a
   a. payments surplus in conjunction with full employment
   b. payments surplus in conjunction with unemployment
   c. payments deficit in conjunction with full employment
   d. payments deficit in conjunction with unemployment

139

9. The policy combination most appropriate for a country operating at full employment with a large trade deficit is
   a. currency appreciation and an increase in government spending
   b. currency depreciation and an increase in government spending
   c. currency depreciation and a decrease in government spending
   d. currency depreciation and a reduction in tax rates

10. The monetary approach suggests that the best way for a nation to reduce a balance-of-payments deficit would be to
    a. devalue its currency
    b. revalue its currency
    c. increase the growth rate of its money supply
    d. decrease the growth rate of its money supply

PROBLEMS AND SHORT ANSWER QUESTIONS

1. Briefly explain why elastic demand for imports and elastic foreign demand for a nation's exports are required for a devaluation of that nation's currency to improve its trade balance. Is this more likely to be the case for a nation that imports specialized equipment available only from a small number of foreign countries, or for a nation with domestic firms that also produce items similar to those imported? Explain.

2. Consider the difference between Japan, which imports most of the raw materials used to produce its manufactured export goods, and the United States, where a much higher percentage of raw materials and other inputs used in export products originate domestically. Explain how a 20 percent appreciation of the yen would have a different effect on the export competitiveness of Japanese firms than would a 20 percent appreciation of the dollar on the export competitiveness of U.S. firms. Which nation would suffer the most from such appreciation?

3.   What is the "J-curve" effect? What important factors explain this time path in response to a currency devaluation? What does this imply about the need for international reserves to finance ongoing trade deficits?

4.   Suppose that, after one country devalues its currency, firms in that country respond to the reduced foreign competition by raising their domestic prices, and export firms in other countries reduce their domestic prices and profit margins in order to minimize loss of market share. Explain how these responses would affect the impact of this devaluation on the first country's trade deficit.

5.   Consider a country that meets the Marshall-Lerner condition and is operating at full employment. If the country devalues its currency in order to correct a trade deficit, explain what macroeconomic policy adjustments also would be necessary in order for the devaluation to be successful.

6.   Both the absorption approach and the monetary approach to exchange rate adjustment predict that a devaluation under conditions of full employment would fail to correct a balance-of-payments deficit. How do these two approaches differ from each other?

EXPLORATIONS BEYOND THE CLASSROOM

1.   Locate a recent newspaper article dealing with currency fluctuations. Can you find evidence that a particular currency recently has depreciated relative to some currencies yet at the same time has appreciated or gained value relative to other currencies? What explanation might be provided for this phenomenon?

2.   Search recent newspaper articles for evidence of the importance of the currency pass-through phenomenon in response to a devaluation or depreciation. What rationale is provided for such response on the part of export firms, and import-competing firms? What impact is this likely to have on the effectiveness of the depreciation?

3.   Locate an example of a government that has attempted to use a depreciation or devaluation to reduce a trade deficit while its economy was operating at or near full employment. What evidence do you find either that the government was required also to use restrictive monetary or fiscal policies to ensure success, or that the absence of such policies led to domestic inflation that made the depreciation ineffective?

4.   Review recent newspapers for articles dealing with countries that have modified their domestic monetary policies in order to deal with balance-of-payments problems. Explain whether the monetary approach to exchange rate adjustment can be used to provide a rationale for such policy changes.

CHAPTER 16

EXCHANGE RATE SYSTEMS

SYNOPSIS OF CHAPTER CONTENT

Although Western nations operated primarily within a system of fixed exchange rates from the end of World War II until the mid-1970s, the present international monetary system provides considerable scope for each nation to choose how the exchange rates between its currency and those of other nations will be determined. The purpose of this chapter is to analyze and evaluate alternative exchange rate systems, and to review historically the exchange rate systems that have prevailed in the past and the choices that individual nations or groups of nations are making today.

One option is **fixed** or **pegged exchange rates**. A nation making this choice would tie the value of its currency to that of a **key currency**. Currencies selected as key currencies generally are actively traded on world money markets, have relatively stable or noninflationary values over time, and are accepted as means of international payment. Fixed exchange rates are used today principally by smaller developing countries, both to stabilize domestic prices of their primary commodity exports whose world prices are set in industrial nation markets and also as an incentive to control domestic inflation in order to maintain the pegged exchange rates. In some cases the exchange rates are tied to individual key currencies such as the U.S. dollar. In other cases, especially when the developing country has important trading links with several different countries, it may peg its currency to a *basket of currencies* that would fluctuate in value by less than would an individual key currency. One frequently used basket is the **special drawing right (SDR)** created by the IMF, whose value is a weighted average of five important key currencies (U.S. dollar, Deutsche mark, Japanese yen, French franc, and Pound sterling).

In a fixed exchange rate system, each participating country determines a **par value** for its currency (in terms of gold, dollars, or SDRs). For example, if Bolivia established a par value of 20 pesos per U.S. dollar and Ecuador set a par value of 10 sucres per U.S. dollar, the **official exchange rate** between these currencies would be 2 pesos to 1 sucre. In order to maintain the par value or official exchange rate of its currency, a nation must establish an **exchange stabilization fund** to defend that value. For instance, if the Bolivian peso began to fall in value to a level such as 22 pesos per U.S. dollar, the Bolivian government would be required to sell dollars or other hard currencies from its reserve fund, buying back pesos and thereby moving the value of the peso back toward its par value of 20 pesos per U.S. dollar. Conversely, a rise in the value of the peso would enable the Bolivian government to supply additional pesos to international currency markets, acquiring dollars or other hard currencies to add to its reserves or exchange stabilization fund.

Although exchange stabilization funds may be used successfully in response to temporary upward or downward exchange rate movements, longer-term changes in basic underlying economic conditions may create a **fundamental disequilibrium** whereby the market exchange rate diverges more permanently from the official rate. For instance, persistent domestic inflation would cause the official exchange rate of a nation's currency to be an overvaluation of its market equilibrium level. One way to correct for this discrepancy would be to eliminate the inflationary pressure through restrictive domestic monetary and fiscal policies. Alternatively, if the government considers such policies to have unacceptable domestic consequences such as high unemployment, it may opt for a **devaluation** of its currency, selecting a new, lower par value at the estimated market equilibrium rate. This legal act of devaluation under a fixed exchange rate system also would cause the nation's currency to **depreciate** or fall in value relative to the currencies of other nations, unless those nations also chose to devalue their currencies by the same percent. A nation that found its currency to be undervalued might carry out a **revaluation**, raising the par value of its currency. This legal act of revaluation also would constitute an **appreciation** or increase in value relative to the currencies of other nations, except for nations that chose to revalue their currencies by the same percent.

Devaluations and revaluations are considered to be **expenditure-switching policies**. For instance, a nation that devalues its currency is attempting to divert or switch the purchases of its own citizens away from the now more expensive imports toward domestic products, and to switch the purchases of people in other nations away from their own products toward the now less expensive exports of the devaluing nation. As we saw in Chapter 15, such expenditure-switching policies will be successful only if demand for imports and exports is sufficiently elastic, as specified in the Marshall-Lerner condition.

Many nations today do not maintain fixed exchange rates but rather allow the values of their currencies to be established according to supply and demand forces in a system of **floating** or **flexible exchange rates**. In such a system, par values and official exchange rates do not exist. Exchange stabilization funds are not required, although governments may utilize such reserves to limit or modify the fluctuations of their currencies in foreign exchange markets. With flexible exchange rates, a rapid growth in U.S. income would increase U.S. demand for imports from countries such as Germany, increase the demand for marks to pay for such imports, and cause the mark to appreciate relative to the dollar; no intervention would be required to purchase the excess supply of dollars in order to maintain a par value of the dollar. Similarly, economic growth in countries such as Germany and Japan would contribute to depreciation of their currencies relative to the dollar, or appreciation of the dollar relative to the mark and the yen.

An advantage of floating exchange rates is that they allow currency values to adjust quickly to new equilibrium levels as underlying economic forces create shifts in supply or demand curves for foreign exchange. Governments need not maintain expensive exchange stabilization funds or distort domestic monetary and fiscal policies in order to support the par values of their currencies, as they would under a fixed exchange rate system. On the other hand, recent experience with floating exchange rates has led to concern among executives of financial and nonfinancial corporations about the extreme volatility of exchange rates and the potentially disruptive effects of such volatility on international trade and capital movements. Yet it is important to remember that the trade barriers and foreign exchange controls often used by governments to support par currency values under a fixed exchange rate regime also create uncertainty and disruption for those engaged in international trade and finance. In addition to concerns about volatility, some critics fear that floating exchange rates eliminate the fiscal and monetary discipline imposed by a fixed exchange rate system and thus contribute to an inflationary bias in the international economy. Evidence on the relative advantages of fixed and flexible exchange rates is mixed, and the debate continues.

From a historical standpoint, after the collapse in the 1930s of the gold standard with its fixed exchange rates, nations became dissatisfied with the resulting instabilities and the resort to nationalistic trade and financial policies that characterized the pre- World War II period. Representatives from United Nations member nations met in 1944 to establish a new international monetary order that became known as the **Bretton Woods system**. Committed to exchange rate stability but recognizing the limitations of fixed exchange rates, the Bretton Woods participants developed a system of **adjustable pegged exchange rates**, a system that remained in effect from 1944 until 1973.

Under the Bretton Woods system, each member nation set a par value for its currency, specified either in terms of gold or of the U.S. dollar, which in turn was tied to gold at $35 per ounce. Currencies were permitted to fluctuate within a 2 percent band, 1 percent above or below par value, and exchange stabilization funds were used by governments to maintain fluctuations within these limits. In 1971 these margins were widened to 2.25 percent above and below parity, in order to facilitate balance of payments adjustment processes and to discourage destabilizing speculation. Member nations facing problems of fundamental disequilibrium in their balance of payments were permitted to repeg their currencies up to 10 percent without permission from the International Monetary Fund, or by greater amounts with such permission; hence, Bretton Woods was known as an "adjustable peg" system. The role of the International Monetary Fund was to monitor the system, to provide or lend reserves to member nations for exchange rate stabilization purposes, to approve devaluations or revaluations of currencies, and to advise national governments regarding domestic policy adjustments needed to restore fundamental exchange rate equilibrium.

The U.S. dollar was the key reserve currency during the Bretton Woods period, and its par value of $35 per ounce of gold was maintained throughout the entire period from 1944 to 1971. However, the Bretton Woods system provided for only limited flexibility, and the strains from persistent disequilibrium situations became increasingly apparent in the late 1960s. After a period of persistent and growing trade deficits, the United States suspended convertibility of the dollar into gold in August 1971, devalued the dollar to $38 per ounce in December 1971, and devalued it again to $43 in February 1973. By late 1973 it was clear that the Bretton Woods system had broken down, and nations no longer retained their commitments to par values or pegged exchange rates.

Since 1973 the United States and many other industrial nations have been operating within a **managed floating system**, with exchange rates allowed to fluctuate according to market forces; at the same time, governments have intervened according to IMF guidelines to preserve orderly market conditions and to prevent excessive short-term exchange rate fluctuations. A **clean float**, influenced only by market supply and demand forces, becomes what some refer to as a **dirty float** because of government intervention to limit exchange rate movements. A policy of **leaning against the wind** would call for governments to prevent erratic short-term fluctuations but not to interfere with longer-term movements of exchange rates to new equilibrium levels. Governments, however, might also choose to resist currency appreciation for domestic policy or international competitiveness reasons. Because there are no formal guidelines for intervention and because summit meetings generally arrive at informal understandings rather than formal agreements, it is difficult to specify exactly the nature and extent of management" in today's floating exchange rate system.

In addition to intervening directly in foreign exchange markets to manage exchange rate fluctuations, governments of course can alter their underlying economic policies in order to influence equilibrium exchange rate movements in a floating exchange rate system. Governments wishing to avoid currency depreciation, for instance, could pursue contractionary monetary policies; governments experiencing currency appreciation could stabilize currency values by expanding their domestic money supplies to meet the strong demand. Such moves may conflict with domestic policy objectives, however, and governments might choose to allow the exchange rate fluctuations to occur.

Within a general system of floating exchange rates, groups or blocs of nations may choose to link their currencies to each other through fixed exchange rates and permit only **joint floating** of their currencies against the currencies of outside nations. The **European Monetary System** (EMS), established in 1979 as an outgrowth of the European Community, involves such an arrangement. The EMS created the **European Currency Unit (ECU)** as an asset to serve as a numeraire for specifying exchange rates among member currencies and as a unit for making balance-of-payments settlements among member central banks. With the **Maastricht Treaty** of 1992, members of the European Community agreed to move toward a more complete **Economic and Monetary Union** with a single European currency and a European central bank to conduct monetary policy. The degree of cooperation and coordination among member nations' monetary and fiscal policies required to maintain stable currency exchange rates has been difficult to sustain; consequently, member nations have been forced to realign their exchange rates on several occasions. The policy coordination required to meet the conditions of the Maastricht Treaty is even more demanding, and it remains to be seen whether member governments are willing to transfer sufficient national sovereignty rights to a supranational European body to achieve this more complete economic and monetary unification. A positive step in this direction was taken by 11 members of the European Union, who agreed to currency unification and introduced the euro as a single currency in January 1999 (national currencies remained in circulation until the year 2002, but at fixed rates relative to the euro).

Other nations have adopted different variations on the spectrum from fixed to flexible exchange rates. Brazil and a few other countries have adopted a version of the adjustable peg, known as the **crawling peg**. Although Brazil maintains a par value, it agreed to make frequent adjustments in this par value, primarily to permit frequent devaluations in the face of significant domestic inflation so as to avoid the consequences of an overvalued currency. Whether this is more similar to the adjustable peg or to managed floating depends on the frequency of adjustment. Frequent changes in par value help to avoid the adverse effects of disequilibrium exchange rates, while less frequent adjustments may provide support for the internal discipline required to keep domestic inflation under control.

Finally, some nations use **exchange controls** to ration the shortage of foreign exchange that results from maintaining overvalued currencies in a pegged exchange rate system. Rather than allowing their currencies to depreciate to restore equilibrium, governments may limit the types of international transactions for which they will authorize domestic individuals or corporations to acquire foreign currency (for instance, payment for imports, tourist expenditures abroad, and repatriation of profits to headquarters in other nations). Alternatively, such governments may limit the amount of foreign exchange that can be acquired for such purposes. Another mechanism for rationing a limited amount of foreign exchange is the practice of **multiple exchange rates**, whereby a government establishes favorable exchange rates for transactions which it wishes to encourage (such as high-priority export or import items) and less favorable exchange rates for activities which it wishes to discourage. Similar to this is a system of **dual exchange rates**, whereby commercial transactions such as import and export activities are financed at a pegged exchange rate, while capital account transactions take place in a financial market where exchange rates are allowed to float freely; the intent is to insulate basic commercial activity from the destabilizing effects of exchange rate fluctuations caused by volatile international capital flows. Governments that attempt to utilize exchange controls or multiple exchange rate systems face significant challenges in making sound decisions about which activities to favor, and in controlling the fraud and corruption arising when firms or individuals attempt to gain access to foreign exchange or favorable exchange rates for which their transactions are not eligible.

KEY CONCEPTS AND TERMS (Define each concept, and briefly explain its significance.)

Fixed exchange rates

Par value

Key currency

Official exchange rate

Fundamental disequilibrium

Exchange stabilization fund

Devaluation, contrasted with depreciation
Revaluation, contrasted with appreciation

Bretton Woods Agreement

Special Drawing Right (SDR)

Adjustable pegged exchange rates

Floating exchange rates

Managed floating system

Clean versus dirty floating

Joint floating

Currency boards

European Monetary System

European Currency Unit

Maastricht Treaty

European Monetary Union, and the euro

Crawling peg

Exchange controls

Multiple exchange rates

Dual exchange rates

TRUE OR FALSE? (On an exam, be prepared to explain *why* the statement is true or false.)

T F 1.　　The Bretton Woods Agreement called for member countries to adopt floating exchange rates.

T F 2.　　The U.S. dollar was a key currency during most of the Bretton Woods period.

T F 3.　　Exchange stabilization funds are used by governments to prevent their currencies from fluctuating by more than a few percentage points above or below par value.

T F 4.　　Under a system of adjustable pegged exchange rates, a government facing persistent balance-of-payments deficits most likely would consider a currency devaluation.

T F 5.　　A devaluation is simply another term for a currency depreciation.

T F 6.　　The term "dirty floating" sometimes is used to describe government use of exchange stabilization funds to influence exchange rates in a floating exchange rate system.

T F 7.　　The Maastricht Treaty calls for members of the European Community to adopt floating exchange rates among their currencies.

T F 8.　　The crawling peg system was used by governments such as Brazil to correct for currency overvaluation caused by high domestic inflation.

T F 9.   The primary purpose of exchange controls is to enable nations with overvalued currencies to ration scarce foreign currency.

T F10.   The term "multiple exchange rates" is used to recognize that in a floating exchange rate system a nation's currency may have many different values over the course of a year.

MULTIPLE CHOICE

1.   The Bretton Woods Agreement called for all the following *except*
      a.   par values
      b.   floating exchange rates
      c.   key currencies
      d.   official exchange rates

2.   If the official exchange rate of the British pound sterling were changed from $2.80 to $2.40 under an adjustable pegged exchange rate system, the pound sterling would be
      a.   revalued and appreciated against the U.S. dollar
      b.   revalued but not appreciated against the U.S. dollar
      c.   devalued and depreciated against the U.S. dollar
      d.   devalued but not depreciated against the U.S. dollar

3.   Key currencies in the 1990s include
      a.   only Special Drawing Rights (SDRs) issued by the IMF
      b.   only currencies with established par values
      c.   currencies so designated by a vote of the United Nations General Assembly
      d.   currencies, such as the U.S. dollar and the Deutsche mark, that are relatively stable in value and widely accepted as means of payment for international transactions

4.   Under the Bretton Woods system, a nation whose currency fell 3 percent below par value would be expected to
      a.   sell more of its own currency on foreign-exchange markets, acquiring additional reserves for its exchange-stabilization fund
      b.   sell reserves from its exchange-stabilization fund
      c.   immediately devalue its currency
      d.   use exchange controls to ration scarce foreign exchange

5.   If Britain devalued the pound sterling by 10 percent against the dollar, and then Japan devalued the yen by 10 percent against the dollar,
      a.   the Japanese action would reverse the pound sterling devaluation against the dollar
      b.   the pound sterling would have depreciated by 10 percent against the dollar and against the yen
      c.   the pound sterling would be devalued by 10 percent against the dollar but would not be depreciated against the yen
      d.   British residents would have incentives to switch their expenditures from Japanese to British goods and services

6.   In comparison with fixed exchange rates, floating exchange rates
      a.   increase the importance of exchange-stabilization funds
      b.   reduce the potential need for costly domestic policy measures to correct a fundamental balance-of-payments disequilibrium
      c.   reduce the need for importers to hedge in forward markets
      d.   require more countries to establish par values for their currencies

149

7. In comparison with freely floating exchange rates, a system of managed floating rates
   a. involves government intervention to limit short-term exchange-rate fluctuations
   b. calls for IMF management to prevent dirty floating
   c. increases exchange-rate instability
   d. reestablishes a system of adjustable pegged exchange rates similar to that of the Bretton Woods system

8. The Maastricht Treaty
   a. allows for more exchange-rate flexibility among European Community member currencies
   b. abolishes the European Currency Unit in favor of the SDR
   c. grants more discretionary authority to central banks in each of the European Community member nations
   d. calls for a move toward more complete economic and monetary union within the European Community

9. Countries use multiple exchange rates primarily in order to
   a. develop trading relationships with many different countries rather than simply with a single partner
   b. move more quickly toward freely floating exchange rates
   c. ration scarce foreign exchange by favoring high-priority uses rather than by depreciating their currencies
   d. facilitate more frequent devaluations, as with Brazil's crawling peg system.

10. Countries adopt dual or two-tier exchange rates in order to
    a. trade with two countries at different exchange rates
    b. provide a stable, pegged exchange rate for commercial or trade transactions while using a floating exchange rate to equilibrate international capital flows
    c. treat fellow members of a regional integration unit such as the EC differently than they treat outside countries
    d. have one exchange rate for imports and another more favorable exchange rate for exports

PROBLEMS AND SHORT ANSWER QUESTIONS

1. What is the difference between par values and official exchange rates under a fixed exchange rate system? If the par value of the British pound sterling were set at $1.50, and the par value of the Japanese yen at $0.01 (100 yen per dollar), what would be the official exchange rate between the pound sterling and the yen?

2.   Suppose that, under the Bretton Woods adjustable peg system, Britain devalued the pound sterling from $1.50 to $1.35, France then devalued the franc from $0.20 to $0.18, and Germany left the mark unchanged at $0.60. Describe how this would affect the exchange rates between the pound sterling and the U.S. dollar, the French franc, and the German mark in terms of depreciation or appreciation. Briefly discuss the probable impact of these adjustments on trade flows among the United States, Britain, France, and Germany.

3.   On the following graph, if S_0 and D_0 represent the initial supply and demand conditions for German marks, what would be the equilibrium exchange rate? Why might rapid economic growth in the United States, coupled with unchanged economic conditions in Germany, cause the demand curve for marks to shift to D_1 while the supply curve remained unchanged? If exchange rates were freely floating, what would happen to the exchange rate? Would the dollar have appreciated or depreciated? If this had occurred during the Bretton Woods period, with a par value set at $0.50 per mark, would the U.S. government have been required to use its exchange-stabilization fund to *buy* marks or to *sell* marks in order to maintain this par value? Show this on the graph, and briefly explain.

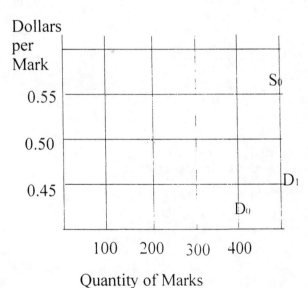

4.	Briefly describe the circumstances that led to the demise of the Bretton Woods system in the late 1960s and early 1970s. What type of exchange-rate system has prevailed since that time?

5.	What is a managed floating exchange-rate system? What lessons have we learned during the last two decades regarding the advantages and the drawbacks of such a system, in comparison with fixed rates?

.

6.	Briefly describe the joint floating system of the European Community. What benefits do EC members derive from this system?

7. What changes has the Maastricht Treaty brought to members of the European Monetary Union? What benefits does it bring to EMU members, and what constraints does it place on member countries regarding independent conduct of national monetary and fiscal policies?

8. Why do some nations adopt multiple or dual exchange rate systems? What potential advantages do these systems offer in comparison with either adjustable peg or freely floating exchange rate systems? What enforcement problems do governments of such nations encounter?

EXPLORATIONS BEYOND THE CLASSROOM

1. Consult recent International Monetary Fund reports to determine the stability or volatility of exchange rates over the past 2 years (a) between the U.S. dollar and currencies of other major industrial nations, (b) among currencies of European Community members, and (c) between currencies of Latin American nations such as Argentina, Brazil or Mexico and the U.S. dollar.

2. Review recent newspaper or magazine reports for information on implementation of the Maastricht Treaty in the European Community. What benefits have EMU members realized since the introduction of the euro? What challenges have individual member countries faced because of the elimination of national monetary policy and the limitations on national fiscal policy?

3. Review news accounts of the economic crises experienced by Southeast Asian nations such as Indonesia and Thailand since 1997. How do these crises reflect the debate over fixed versus flexible exchange rates, and the debate over whether such countries should adopt currency boards?

CHAPTER 17

MACROECONOMIC POLICY IN AN OPEN ECONOMY

SYNOPSIS OF CHAPTER CONTENT

National governments are committed primarily to maintaining full employment and price stability within their own domestic economies. The process of achieving these goals becomes more complicated when such domestic economies are linked to the outside world through trade and financial flows, and when national governments must be concerned not only with domestic objectives but also with maintaining balance-of-payments (BOP) equilibrium. This chapter deals with the process of pursuing both domestic and international economic objectives, and the importance of economic policy cooperation among national governments as each strives to meet its own goals.

International economic policy refers not only to government policies with obvious direct international effects, such as the use of import tariffs and quotas, but also to more general monetary and fiscal policy decisions that have at least indirect international consequences. Policies usually do not fit easily into simple categories, but rather fall somewhere along a continuum between those with primarily internal effects and those with primarily external consequences. Governments seek to achieve **internal balance**, usually defined as an optimal combination of closeness to full employment and reasonable domestic price stability (absence of inflation). National governments also must be cognizant of **external balance** considerations, or the need to maintain BOP equilibrium. Such equilibrium can be thought of in terms of overall balance including both current and capital accounts (for instance, a current account deficit offset by an equal capital account surplus), but often nations also perceive a need to avoid persistent current account deficits or to achieve trade balance, with exports equal to imports.

National policies that increase or decrease the total level of demand or expenditures within the domestic economy can be classified as **expenditure-changing policies**. These include **fiscal policy** (changes in government spending or in taxes) and **monetary policy** (changes in the nation's money supply and interest rates). The standard response to problems of excessive unemployment is to increase aggregate demand through expansionary fiscal or monetary policy (more government spending, lower taxes, or an increased money supply and lower interest rates). Alternatively, excessive inflation calls for restrictive fiscal or monetary policies (reduced government spending, higher taxes, or a reduced money supply and higher interest rates).

Policies designed to modify or shift the *direction* of demand are classified as **expenditure-switching policies**. For example, a nation with a trade deficit could devalue its currency under a fixed exchange-rate system or encourage its currency to depreciate under a flexible exchange-rate system in order to encourage domestic and foreign residents to switch their purchases away from goods and services produced abroad toward those produced within that country, thereby increasing exports and reducing imports. Thus, **exchange-rate adjustments** constitute the primary form of expenditure-switching policies. National governments also may use **direct controls** over trade (import tariffs, quotas, limits on tourist spending) or over capital flows (limits on foreign investment, taxes on foreign interest income) in order to reduce a BOP deficit.

A nation is considered to have achieved **overall balance** when it has reached both internal balance with respect to unemployment and inflation and external balance with respect to BOP equilibrium. Efforts to achieve such balance can involve both expenditure-switching and expenditure-changing policies. For instance, a nation with both domestic recession and a BOP deficit might adopt an expenditure-switching policy of devaluing its currency or allowing it to depreciate; the primary impact would be to reduce the nation's trade deficit, but secondarily the increase in net exports also would stimulate demand and bring the domestic economy closer to full employment. Likewise, a currency revaluation or appreciation would help restore both external and internal balance for a nation experiencing domestic inflation and a BOP surplus. However, nations in other circumstances would face policy dilemmas; a country with a

BOP deficit coupled with an overheated economy and domestic inflation would find that an expenditure-switching policy of currency devaluation would at least temporarily reduce its trade deficit but only intensify its internal problems with inflation. Thus, nations sometimes may need to accompany expenditure-switching policies with expenditure-reducing policies in order to succeed.

It also is important to consider how expenditure-changing policies would affect overall balance. The primary impact of such policies, particularly monetary and fiscal policies, is on a nation's internal balance. However, monetary and fiscal policies also will affect external balance, especially to the extent that international capital flows are sensitive to interest-rate differentials between countries. Fiscal policy expansion to correct a domestic recession would move an economy closer to full employment but would also increase domestic interest rates as the economic expansion increased demand for money. With fixed exchange rates, this probably would create a BOP surplus as capital inflows exceeded the tendency toward a current account deficit when imports rose with the domestic expansion. Monetary authorities would purchase foreign currency reserves in exchange for domestic currency, to prevent the domestic currency from appreciating, thus reinforcing the domestic economic recovery. However, with flexible or floating exchange rates the outcome would not be so successful, because the BOP surplus created by the fiscal expansion would cause the domestic currency to appreciate, and the resulting negative impact on net exports would nullify the intended positive impact of the fiscal stimulus on the domestic economy.

The effects of monetary policy can be analyzed in a similar fashion. With fixed exchange rates, a monetary expansion to promote economic recovery would increase income and also reduce interest rates; the higher income would contribute to a current account or trade deficit, while the lower interest rates would create capital outflows and a capital account deficit. The resulting BOP deficit would require monetary authorities to sell reserves and acquire domestic currency in order to prevent a depreciation, thereby reversing the initial monetary expansion and pushing the economy back into recession. However, if exchange rates were flexible, the BOP deficit resulting from monetary expansion would lead to a currency depreciation, which in turn would increase net exports and reinforce the positive impact of monetary expansion on the domestic economy.

In summary, fiscal policy is effective in restoring internal balance when exchange rates are fixed, but loses its effectiveness under a flexible exchange-rate system. Monetary policy, alternatively, can be used effectively to restore internal balance when exchange rates are allowed to fluctuate but loses its effectiveness under a fixed exchange-rate system.

The impact of fiscal and monetary policy on external balance is relevant only under a fixed exchange-rate system, because with flexible rates external balance is ensured by exchange-rate adjustment. With fixed exchange rates, monetary expansion clearly would worsen both the current and capital accounts, as explained above. In essence, this is why monetary policy should not be used to restore internal balance, because the resulting BOP deficit would call for an immediate monetary contraction, reversing the initial benefits from monetary expansion. The external balance effects of fiscal expansion are more ambiguous. Fiscal expansion to eliminate a recession would increase domestic income and thus contribute to a trade deficit, but it also would put upward pressure on interest rates and attract capital from abroad. In the short term, the net effect may well be to generate a BOP surplus if capital is highly mobile; however, later repayment of interest and profits will moderate or reverse the capital account surplus, and the trade deficit itself may be viewed negatively from a policy standpoint.

Under a fixed or pegged exchange-rate system, monetary policy may be able to deal effectively with certain combinations of internal and external imbalance. For instance, a nation with domestic unemployment and a BOP surplus could use expansionary monetary policy that would simultaneously restore both full employment and external balance. Likewise, a restrictive monetary policy would be effective in an economy with high inflation and a BOP deficit. However, a **policy conflict** would exist in an economy with high inflation and a BOP surplus; restrictive monetary policy to fight inflation would increase the surplus, and expansionary monetary policy to reduce the surplus would intensify the inflation. In such a situation, governments most often choose to fight inflation and restore domestic equilibrium, allowing the BOP surplus to persist despite the implied BOP deficits for other nations. A more painful policy conflict exists when an economy experiences both domestic recession and a BOP deficit; expansionary monetary policy to restore full employment would intensify the BOP deficit, while restrictive monetary policy to reduce the BOP deficit would deepen the recession.

Because the BOP effects of fiscal policy are ambiguous, it is not clear whether the use of fiscal rather than monetary policy would enable a nation to avoid these policy conflicts. However, a combination of expansionary monetary or fiscal policy to promote recovery from domestic recession and a devaluation to reduce a BOP deficit might help resolve the policy conflict discussed above, as long as inflation is kept in check. Import tariffs or quotas also might be used to restore external balance, although such use of trade barriers would conflict with the GATT (now WTO) commitment to move toward freer trade. In the early 1960s the U.S. Federal Reserve Board attempted to raise short-term interest rates to attract capital from abroad while reducing long-term interest rates to stimulate domestic investment. **Operation Twist**, so named because of the effort to twist the yield curve, had only moderate success because of the Fed's limited ability to change the relationships among short-term and long-term interest rates. Further complications arise if nations simultaneously face recession, inflation, and a BOP deficit; three distinct problems call for three rather than two policy targets. Faced with such circumstances in 1971, the United States chose to address the recession with expansionary macroeconomic policies, control inflation with wage and price controls, and reduce the BOP deficit with a devaluation of the dollar. The dilemma was very real, but the effectiveness of wage and price controls was limited and temporary.

Economic relations among nations can range from *open conflict* to complete *integration*. The latter would occur, for instance, among EC members if they moved through the Maastricht Treaty process to achieve complete economic and monetary union, transferring authority for policymaking from national governments to regional institutions. Most nations find themselves somewhere along the spectrum between *policy independence*, allowing each nation to operate independently and without consultation, and *integration*.

International economic policy coordination can take a variety of forms. Government leaders from several nations can gather at summit meetings to discuss domestic and international concerns, as with the **Smithsonian Agreement** of 1971, where leaders from major industrial nations met to realign exchange rates. This was a temporarily successful effort to preserve the fixed exchange rate structure of the Bretton Woods system, which ultimately disintegrated in 1973. At the 1978 **Bonn Summit**, Germany and Japan agreed to stimulate their domestic economies while the United States agreed to raise domestic oil prices to world levels, in an effort to reduce U.S. trade deficits and German and Japanese trade surpluses. Participants in the **Plaza Accord** of 1985 agreed to modify domestic monetary and fiscal policies and to intervene in foreign exchange markets in order to reverse the strong appreciation of the dollar that had occurred between 1980 and 1985. Finally, industrial nations agreed through the **Louvre Accord** in 1987 to engage in managed floating to stabilize the exchange rates among their currencies. In each case, the degree of success depended more on the willingness of participating nations to alter their fundamental macroeconomic policies than on the formal statements made in support of exchange-rate targets or government interventions in currency markets.

Economic policymakers from the major industrial nations also meet regularly through ongoing institutions or forums such as the **International Monetary Fund (IMF)**, the **Organization for Economic Cooperation and Development (OECD)**, and the **Group of Seven (G-7)**; the Group of Seven, representing the world's seven largest industrial nations, is of sufficient importance that members now are discussing its possible expansion to include additional newly industrialized states.

Under some circumstances the domestic and international objectives of different national governments coincide with each other, and policy coordination is easy to achieve. For instance, if two nations each had domestic recession and BOP equilibrium, they would be reluctant to expand their economies independently of each other, for fear of creating trade deficits; however, through coordinated expansions both nations could achieve full employment while increasing exports and imports, thus maintaining BOP equilibrium. Furthermore, coordinated efforts to use either monetary or fiscal policy to promote domestic expansion could avoid the undesired international capital flows that would arise if interest-rate

156

differentials increased because one nation used monetary policy while the other used fiscal policy. However, because nations often are in conflicting circumstances and each has multiple domestic goals or constraints, such smooth international economic policy coordination often is difficult to achieve in practice.

KEY CONCEPTS AND TERMS (Define each concept, and briefly explain its significance.)

International economic policy

Internal balance

External balance

Expenditure-switching policies

Expenditure-changing policies

Direct controls

Overall balance

Policy conflicts and agreements

Operation Twist

157

International economic policy coordination

Smithsonian Agreement

Bonn Summit Agreement

Plaza Accord

Louvre Accord

Organization for Economic Cooperation and Development (OECD)

Group of Seven (G-7)

TRUE OR FALSE? (On an exam, be prepared to explain *why* the statement is true or false.)

T F 1. Internal balance refers to trade balance between members of a regional economic integration unit.

T F 2. External balance occurs when a nation has neither an overall balance-of-payments deficit nor a surplus

T F 3. A currency devaluation or depreciation is an example of an expenditure-changing policy.

T F 4. A reduction in government spending is an example of an expenditure-changing policy.

T F 5. Under fixed exchange rates, monetary expansion would help a nation with a recession and a BOP deficit solve both problems.

T F 6. A nation with a recession and a BOP deficit could help solve both problems by depreciating its currency.

T F 7.   Operation Twist refers to efforts by one national government to convince another nation to devalue its currency.

T F 8.   The Smithsonian Agreement was a coordinated effort by major industrial nations to adjust their exchange rates in 1971.

T F 9.   The Group of Seven is an organization of developing countries in Latin America.

T F10.   The Plaza Accord was an agreement among major industrial nations to return to the Bretton Woods fixed exchange-rate system in 1985.

MULTIPLE CHOICE

1.   One clear sign that a nation has not achieved internal balance is
    a.   a persistent BOP deficit
    b.   a depreciation of its currency in foreign exchange markets
    c.   capital inflows from other nations
    d.   high domestic unemployment and slow GDP growth

2.   An expenditure-switching policy is designed primarily to
    a.   switch domestic spending to higher-productivity items
    b.   reduce a persistent BOP deficit
    c.   reduce domestic inflationary pressure
    d.   reduce domestic interest rates

3.   An example of an expenditure-switching policy would be
    a.   an increase in the domestic money supply
    b.   an increase in a nation's government spending
    c.   a devaluation of a nation's currency
    d.   lower income tax rates to promote economic recovery

4.   One policy that would help a nation recover from recession and reduce a BOP deficit is
    a.   a depreciation of the nation's currency
    b.   an appreciation of the nation's currency
    c.   an increase in the nation's money supply
    d.   a reduction in the nation's money supply

5.   Under conditions of fixed exchange rates and high capital mobility, a nation could best promote recovery from recession by
    a.   increasing its money supply
    b.   increasing government spending
    c.   reducing its money supply
    d.   reducing government spending

6.   Under conditions of flexible exchange rates and high capital mobility, a nation could best promote recovery from recession by
    a.   increasing its money supply
    b.   increasing government spending
    c.   reducing its money supply
    d.   reducing government spending

159

7.   A combination of policies that might help a nation both recover from recession and reduce a BOP deficit would be
       a.   monetary contraction and currency revaluation
       b.   monetary contraction and currency devaluation
       c.   monetary expansion and currency revaluation
       d.   monetary expansion and currency devaluation

8.   The 1971 decision by major industrial nations to realign their currency exchange values to promote external balance was
       a.   the Bonn Summit Agreement
       b.   the Louvre Accord
       c.   the Plaza Accord
       d.   the Smithsonian Agreement

9.   The 1985 agreement among industrial nations to intervene in foreign exchange markets to support a depreciation of the U.S. dollar was
       a.   the Bonn Summit Agreement
       b.   the Louvre Accord
       c.   the Plaza Accord
       d.   the Smithsonian Agreement

10.   Under conditions of fixed or stable exchange rates, the circumstances that would be most conducive to international economic policy coordination between Germany and the United States are
       a.   inflation and BOP surplus in Germany, recession and BOP deficit in the United States
       b.   internal balance and BOP surplus in Germany, internal balance and BOP deficit in the United States
       c.   inflation and external balance in Germany, recession and external balance in the United States
       d.   recession and external balance in Germany, recession and external balance in the United States

PROBLEMS AND SHORT ANSWER QUESTIONS

1.   Suppose that a nation, operating within a fixed exchange-rate system, faces both domestic recession and a BOP deficit. Characterize this situation in terms of internal and external balance. Explain why this nation would face a dilemma if it attempted to use monetary policy to restore internal and external balance.

2.   In the situation in Question 1, explain how and why fiscal policy would be more effective than monetary policy in restoring internal balance. Why is the impact of fiscal expansion on the BOP deficit less clear? Under what circumstances would fiscal expansion be most likely also to contribute to restoring external balance for this nation?

3.   Explain the basic difference between expenditure-switching and expenditure-changing policies. Why are expenditure-switching policies more effective in restoring external balance, and expenditure-changing policies better for restoring internal balance?

4.   Suppose that a nation had an economy operating at full employment but with a large BOP deficit. Explain how a combination of expenditure-switching and expenditure-reducing policies might be required to achieve internal and external balance. How does this relate to the absorption approach to BOP adjustment?

5. In the early 1970s the United States moved from a fixed to a flexible exchange-rate system. Explain how this would alter the relative effectiveness of monetary and fiscal policy in promoting recovery from domestic recession.

6. Contrast the Smithsonian Agreement and the Plaza Accord as examples of international economic policy coordination. How does one of these agreements represent cooperation within a pegged exchange-rate system, and the other illustrate managed floating within a flexible exchange-rate system?

7. Give one example of a situation that would lend itself to effective cooperation between Japan and the United States as each tried to achieve internal and external balance, and another set of circumstances which would make it very difficult to achieve such economic policy coordination between these two countries. Explain your reasoning.

8.   In May of 1994, the Japanese government agreed to expand its domestic money supply. The Japanese economy was in recession, Japan had a BOP surplus while the United States had a BOP deficit, and both countries wished to avoid a further appreciation of the Japanese yen. Explain whether this policy move by Japan is likely to help restore internal and external balance in Japan, and whether it is an example of international economic policy coordination between Japan and the United States.

EXPLORATIONS BEYOND THE CLASSROOM

1.   Locate newspaper articles that discuss efforts by governments of major industrial nations such as Germany, Japan, and the United States to deal with balance-of-payments problems. Analyze each nation's situation in terms of internal and external balance issues. What prospects for international policy coordination can you identify? What tensions or conflicts appear to make such coordination difficult to achieve? Why?

2.   Consult publications such as *The Economist* or European newspapers for articles dealing with economic policy formation among members of the European Community. How do the policy debates illustrate the challenges of achieving international economic policy coordination under conditions of fixed exchange rates? What strains, if any, are apparent as EC members try to meet the conditions of the Maastricht Treaty while also pursuing domestic economic goals?

3.   Review recent publications of the IMF or the OECD, or news articles about the Group of Seven or Group of Five meetings. What evidence of successes or remaining challenges do you find regarding efforts to achieve international economic policy cooperation among the major industrial nations? What indications, if any, do you find that the needs or interests of developing countries are being considered in these deliberations among industrial nations?

CHAPTER 18

INTERNATIONAL BANKING: RESERVES, DEBT, AND RISK

SYNOPSIS OF CHAPTER CONTENT

International banking plays an important role in financing international trade, in funding international investment and other capital flows among countries, and in facilitating balance-of-payments adjustment. This chapter explores the function of the International Monetary Fund and national central banks in this process, the activities of private commercial banks, and the ways in which these public and private institutions have contributed to both the origins and the resolutions of the international debt problems of developing countries.

As we have seen in previous chapters, the central banks of national governments hold **international reserves** to bridge gaps between international monetary receipts and payments, or to finance balance-of-payments (BOP) deficits. A nation's need for such reserves increases with the volume of its international trade and investment activities, and thus tends to increase as the nation's GDP rises and as its degree of openness within the global economy grows. Another important determinant of the need for international reserves is the exchange-rate system; nations within a fixed exchange-rate system need abundant reserves in order to finance BOP deficits while they gradually make internal policy adjustments to achieve external balance, whereas within a flexible exchange-rate system the need for such reserve assets is much smaller because exchange-rate movements are expected more quickly and smoothly to achieve BOP equilibrium. Under a freely floating exchange-rate system the need for international reserves theoretically would be nonexistent, although phenomena such as the J-curve (delayed response to exchange-rate movements) and government efforts to manage or moderate exchange-rate fluctuations ensure a continuing role for reserve assets.

Other factors that would increase the demand for international reserves include the extent to which automatic domestic adjustment mechanisms to correct BOP disequilibria (domestic price level changes, interest rate changes, income changes) function slowly or incompletely. Domestic constraints or internal policy conflicts that limit the responsiveness of government policies to BOP problems also increase the need for reserves. Finally, difficulties in achieving international economic policy coordination to correct external imbalances, or time lags in negotiating such cooperation among national governments, also increase the need for international reserve assets.

The **supply of international reserve assets** available to governments includes **gold**, **International Monetary Fund (IMF) quotas** or reserve positions, **special drawing rights (SDRs)** issued by the IMF, and holdings of those foreign currencies that have sufficient stability and convertibility to be regarded as **reserve** or **key currencies**. Today nearly 90 percent of total reserves are in the form of key currency or foreign exchange holdings, with the U.S. dollar being the dominant reserve currency held by other governments.

Prior to World War I, the pound sterling was the primary reserve currency, owing to the prominent role of Britain in international trade and of London as an international finance center. Circumstances changed during the Great Depression of the 1930s, and as the United States emerged as the strongest economy after World War II the dollar came to play an increasingly important role as a reserve asset. The decade of the 1950s was known as a *dollar-shortage era* because the demand for U.S. exports generally exceeded the ability of other nations to pay for those products with their own exports. By the early 1960s this had shifted to a situation of *dollar glut*, as persistent U.S. trade deficits gave rise to outflows of dollars that exceeded the demand for such dollars to pay for other nations' imports. By 1970 the value of dollar liabilities in the hands of foreigners was several times as large as total U.S. reserve assets, and the ability of the U.S. government to convert foreign official holdings of dollars into gold was called into question. The dilemma created by this situation became known as the **liquidity problem**, as the mechanism by which the United States was providing liquidity or reserve assets for other nations necessarily involved persistent current account or trade deficits: correcting or eliminating the U.S. trade deficits would also dry up the primary source of reserve assets for the rest of the world.

National currencies such as the U.S. dollar had not always played such a prominent role in creating international liquidity. Under the historic international **gold standard**, which saw its greatest strength from 1880 to 1914, par values of national currencies were established in terms of gold, and paper currencies were backed by gold to ensure their integrity and to provide discipline for national monetary policies. But as paper currency and demand deposits grew in importance, gold as a share of domestic money supplies fell dramatically in the United States and other industrial nations. After World War II, with the establishment of the International Monetary Fund, major industrial nations adopted a **gold exchange standard** in which gold retained a role as a unit of account from the standpoint of currency par values but the dollar was expected to compensate for the relative scarcity of gold as a reserve asset by providing the major source of additional international reserves. During the period of dollar glut in the 1960s the United States was reluctant to devalue the dollar because to do so would have jeopardized confidence in the international monetary system and would have penalized nations that had been willing to hold their reserves primarily in the form of dollars rather than demanding gold from the U.S. Treasury. By 1971 the official U.S. gold stock was only a small fraction of U.S. liabilities to foreign central banks. In August the United States suspended its commitment to convert foreign official dollar holdings into gold, later devalued the dollar from its long-time value of $35 per ounce of gold, and again devalued the dollar in 1973 as the world effectively moved from the gold exchange standard and the adjustable pegged exchange rates of the Bretton Woods period to a system of flexible or floating exchange rates.

In 1970, shortly before the end of the Bretton Woods period, the IMF created a new international reserve asset, the **special drawing right (SDR)**. The SDR, also known as "paper gold," was intended to supplement gold as a reserve asset and to provide an alternative to national currencies such as the U.S. dollar, one that would be under international management rather than controlled by a single national government. Unlike dollar reserves, which grew simply as a reflection of U.S. trade deficits, SDRs could be created by the IMF and allocated as reserves to member nations as the need for international liquidity grew from year to year. Although SDR allocations cannot be used directly by IMF member nations to finance balance-of-payments deficits, subject to certain conditions central banks can convert their SDR holdings into reserve currencies, which in turn can be used for BOP purposes. The SDR initially was tied to the U.S. dollar, but in 1974 a method of **basket valuation** was introduced to determine the worth of the SDR. As a basket currency the SDR value was set as a weighted average of the values of the U.S. dollar, German mark, Japanese yen, French franc, and British pound, thus making it more stable than if it were tied to any single currency. This stability also has made the SDR an attractive unit of account for denominating private commercial or financial transactions. Another advantage of the SDR is that the **seigniorage**, or value of resources transferred to the issuer of new money, can be distributed more equitably among IMF members rather than arbitrarily going either to the United States as creator of additional dollar reserves or to gold-producing nations to the extent that they profit from supplying gold as official reserve assets. Although the SDR today represents less than 3 per cent of global reserve assets, its introduction represents an important step toward the orderly creation of global liquidity by an official international institution, the IMF.

In addition to international reserve assets that are *owned* by national central banks, nations also may have access to various facilities for *borrowing* reserves to help finance balance-of-payments deficits. Deficit nations may acquire foreign currencies through **drawings** on the International Monetary Fund, using up to 50 percent of their own quotas with the Fund to purchase foreign exchange for BOP purposes, and amounts beyond that level with permission or approval of the IMF. Such purchases are intended to be temporary and to be reversed once BOP equilibrium is established, and IMF approval of drawings beyond the 50 percent limit generally is conditional on the nation presenting an acceptable plan for resolving persistent BOP problems. Another source of reserves is the **General Arrangements to Borrow**, established in 1962 by ten industrial nations (the Group of Ten) that agreed to lend up to $6 billion to the IMF if the Fund's stock of foreign currencies became temporarily exhausted. In 1963 the IMF established a **compensatory financing facility** to assist developing nations with BOP problems caused by fluctuations in earnings from primary commodity exports, in 1969 it formed a **buffer stock**

facility to support efforts of developing nations to stabilize primary commodity prices, and in 1974 it created an **oil facility** to help nations weather the effects of OPEC oil price increases. Beyond these IMF initiatives, individual national central banks also have entered into bilateral **swap arrangements**, agreeing to lend or temporarily swap currencies with each other so that one central bank can gain access to a reserve currency in order to finance temporary BOP deficits or to support its own currency's value in foreign exchange markets.

Another important development is the growing role of private commercial banks in international financial markets. Not only do banks making international loans need to assess the **credit (financial) risk** of loan repayment as they would with domestic loans; they also must evaluate the **country (political) risk** related to government policy decisions that could restrict profits or expropriate foreign assets, and must estimate the **currency (economic) risk** associated with currency depreciations, appreciations, or exchange controls imposed by foreign governments. Several organizations develop and market political, economic, and composite risk ratings for individual countries to assist commercial banks in evaluating potential loans to private or public entities within countries around the world.

A significant example of issues arising from international banking is the **international debt problem** of recent decades. Originating with the OPEC oil price shocks of the mid- and late 1970s, many of the "petrodollars" earned by OPEC oil exporters were deposited in U.S. commercial banks and then recycled or lent to borrowers in Latin America. The recession in the U.S. economy coupled with continuing strong growth and loan demand in Latin America made such loans attractive to U.S. banks with excess funds. Although such loans may have appeared prudent at the time, slow growth of the U.S. economy and other industrial economies along with rapid, inflationary growth in Latin America combined to reduce the export earnings of the borrowing nations. Whether measured by the **debt-to-export ratio** (external debt relative to export earnings) or the **debt/service ratio** (interest and principle repayment obligations relative to export earnings), the debt burdens of major borrowers had become excessive by the mid 1980s. The rising value of the dollar from 1980 to 1985 increased the local-currency cost of repaying the dollar-denominated debt, and the refinancing of the unpaid debt at the sharply higher interest rates of the 1980s further increased the burdens of Latin American debtor nations. The external debt of all developing nations approached $1.5 trillion, while individual Latin American nations such as Brazil and Mexico each owed approximately $100 billion, primarily to private U.S. banks.

Several options exist for making these debt burdens more manageable. Debtor nations may cease or delay repayments, or even repudiate or default on their debts; countries such as Brazil and Mexico hesitated to take extreme action because such actions would jeopardize their credit ratings for future loans. The IMF and the World Bank became involved in negotiations, dealing on the one hand with the commercial banks to reschedule and modify loan terms and on the other hand with governments of debtor nations to adopt often-painful internal reform measures. The IMF often insisted on **conditionality**, asking debtor nations to undertake austerity programs in exchange for IMF loans. Some approaches, such as the Brady Initiative of 1989, sought **debt reduction** by commercial banks as a key element of a workable solution. Some advocates of debt relief went further, pressing for **debt forgiveness**, but others responded that this would not guarantee the needed internal reforms and would reward or aid nations that were not among the poorest developing countries. The banks themselves took certain actions to reduce their exposure. Some established loss reserves, some sold their debts to other banks (often at discounts of 70 percent or more) or to the issuing governments as **debt buybacks** (also at discounts), and others engaged in **debt/equity swaps** by accepting equity or ownership positions in debtor-nation assets (local corporations, land or natural resource assets). Solutions often were complex, and tailored to each individual case. International lending can be beneficial to both parties, but the financial losses and social and economic pain generated by the Latin American debt problems have left both bankers and borrowers more cautious about the risks involved.

A final dimension of international banking that deserves mention is the **Eurocurrency market**. This term originally referred to dollar-denominated deposits (**Eurodollars**) in banks (**Eurobanks**) outside the United States. Such terminology is somewhat misleading, because the market includes foreign currencies other than the dollar and includes non-European financial centers such as Hong Kong and Singapore.

Broadly defined, this market includes all deposits denominated in currencies other than those of the country in which the participating bank is located. The market has grown rapidly, for reasons ranging from the efficient financing of international trade to avoidance of interest-rate restrictions, bank reserve requirements, and potential freezing of financial assets imposed by national governments on their own domestic banks. The development of the Eurocurrency market has increased the efficiency and global integration of international capital markets and reduced the need for official reserve assets, and certainly has increased international capital mobility. Some fear that it may also have reduced control of national governments over domestic monetary policies and increased the risk of global financial instability by leaving important commercial financial institutions beyond the control or regulation of government monetary authorities.

KEY CONCEPTS AND TERMS (Define each concept, and briefly explain its significance.)

International reserves

Demand for international reserves

Supply of international reserves

Key (reserve) currencies

International Monetary Fund

IMF quotas, drawings

Special drawing rights (SDRs)

Gold standard

167

Gold exchange standard

Dollar shortage, dollar glut

Liquidity problem with the dollar as a reserve currency

Seigniorage

Demonetization of gold, end of Bretton Woods system

General Arrangements to Borrow

Compensatory financing facility

Buffer stock facility

Oil facility

Swap arrangements

Credit (financial) risk

Country (political) risk

Currency (economic) risk

International debt problem

Debt-to-export ratio

Debt/service ratio

Conditionality

Debt reduction, debt forgiveness

Debt/equity swaps

Eurocurrency market

TRUE OR FALSE? (On an exam, be prepared to explain *why* the statement is true or false.)

T F 1. The demand for international reserves is greater under a flexible than under a fixed exchange-rate system.

T F 2. Today, gold accounts for the highest percentage of official reserve assets held by central banks.

T F 3. The dollar became the most important reserve or key currency after World War II, primarily because of the strength of the U.S. economy and the stability and convertibility of the dollar.

T F 4. A liquidity problem intensified in the 1960s, as the U.S. dollar was able to provide increased global liquidity only if the United States experienced persistent trade deficits.

T F 5. Seigniorage refers to the dollar displacing the pound sterling as a reserve asset because of an aging British economy.

T F 6. Special drawing rights represent access to additional reserve assets created by the International Monetary Fund.

T F 7. The IMF created the oil facility in the 1970s to help OPEC nations finance the construction of oil refineries.

T F 8. The international debt problem originated as U.S. banks made large loans to very poor African nations in the 1970s.

T F 9. "Debt/equity swaps" is another term for debt forgiveness.

T F10. The Eurocurrency market consists of commercial bank deposits that are denominated in currencies other than that of the country in whose banks the deposits are placed.

MULTIPLE CHOICE

1. A factor that would *increase* the demand for international reserves is
   a. increased domestic price flexibility within industrial nations
   b. a reduction in the ratio of exports to GDP for major industrial nations
   c. a shift from a flexible to a fixed exchange-rate system
   d. increased use of import tariffs and exchange controls to reduce balance-of-payments deficits

2. Under the gold exchange standard or the Bretton Woods system, the primary source of increased global liquidity or reserves was
   a. official gold holdings
   b. the U.S. dollar
   c. the British pound sterling
   d. IMF special drawing rights (SDRs)

3. The international liquidity problem of the 1960s refers to
   a. the continuing problem from the 1950s of dollar shortages
   b. the reductions in domestic money supplies among major industrial nations
   c. the refusal of the Fed to convert foreign official holdings of dollars into gold
   d. the dilemma that providing global liquidity also required the United States to run persistent trade deficits

170

4.	The revenue or purchasing power that the United States received by supplying dollars as reserve assets for other nations during the 1960s is known as
	a.	seigniorage
	b.	patronage
	c.	conditionality
	d.	drawing rights

5.	Swap arrangements among national central banks
	a.	enable central banks to convert debt into equity
	b.	exist only under conditions of clean floating or completely flexible exchange rates
	c.	enable central banks to exchange currencies temporarily with other central banks in order to support the values of their own currencies
	d.	enable central banks to exchange key officials with each other so they can more effectively achieve international economic policy coordination

6.	Drawing rights with the International Monetary Fund
	a.	enable central banks to use up to 50 percent of their IMF quotas to acquire reserve currencies to facilitate BOP adjustment
	b.	refer to the General Arrangements to Borrow
	c.	refer to the oil facility established by the IMF
	d.	enable central banks to convert reserve currencies into gold with the IMF

7.	The risk incurred if a U.S. bank lends money to a firm in Haiti. and the Haitian government then nationalizes that firm after a government takeover by the military. is known as
	a.	credit risk
	b.	political or country risk
	c.	currency or economic risk
	d.	conditionality

8.	The international debt crisis of the 1970s and 1980s arose primarily from
	a.	IMF buffer stock loans to Asian nations
	b.	the collapse of major U.S. firms which had borrowed money from Japanese banks
	c.	loans of recycled petrodollars by U.S. banks to industrializing nations in Latin America
	d.	the collapse of the Soviet Union

9.	The practice of U.S. banks exchanging their holdings of loans to Latin American governments or companies for ownership rights in Latin American corporations is known as
	a.	debt forgiveness
	b.	debt/equity swaps
	c.	the Brady Initiative
	d.	demonetization

10.	Factors that have contributed to the rapid growth of the Eurocurrency market include all of the following *except*
	a.	a growing volume of international trade and foreign investment
	b.	domestic interest-rate controls imposed by national governments
	c.	reserve requirements established by national central banks
	d.	the 1973 Federal Reserve System exemption of large-denomination certificates of deposit from Regulation Q ceilings

PROBLEMS AND SHORT ANSWER QUESTIONS

1.   What functions are performed by international reserves? How and why has the relative importance of different international reserve assets changed during the twentieth century?

2.   What has been the role of the U.S. dollar as a key or reserve currency since 1945? How did the United States function as provider of global liquidity or banker for the world? What special problems or dilemmas did this create from the standpoint of (a) seigniorage and (b) U.S. balance-of-payments conditions during the 1960s?

3.   How did the end of the Bretton Woods system in the early 1970s affect the need for international reserve assets? Why is there a continuing need for reserves even with floating exchange rates?

4. In what ways does the IMF provide access to reserves for nations facing BOP problems? Outline the IMF facilities developed particularly for developing countries during the 1960s and 1970s.

5. What are IMF special drawing rights (SDRs)? How are they used? In what ways does the creation of SDRs represent a potentially important alternative to national currencies as international reserve assets?

6. What political and currency risks do commercial banks encounter when they make international loans? What services and strategies are available to help banks cope with these risks?

7.   What major factors contributed to the Latin American debt crisis of the 1970s and 1980s? What are the roles or responsibilities of the commercial banks, the governments of the United States and other industrial nations, the IMF and the World Bank, and the debtor nations themselves in working to resolve these debt problems?

8.   How has increased international capital activity contributed to the East Asian financial crisis of 1997 and 1998? Why has this led some to call for greater regulation of such capital flows, and others to go as far as to suggest that the IMF should be abolished?

9.   What is the Eurocurrency market? How and where does it function? What advantages does it offer for international trade and finance? What potential problems does it pose regarding the stability of the international financial system?

EXPLORATIONS BEYOND THE CLASSROOM

1. Consult recent IMF publications (e.g., *IMF Survey, Finance & Development*) for articles dealing with countries working to resolve balance-of-payments problems. What role is the IMF playing in providing access to reserves? Is the IMF imposing conditionality terms on this access, or otherwise advising national governments about internal adjustment measures that they should adopt?

2. Locate recent articles dealing with IMF loans to low-income developing countries with balance-of-payments problems. How has the IMF responded to concerns that the conditionality terms for such loans be structured in ways that will not harm the poor or most vulnerable groups within those nations?

3. Locate recent newspaper or magazine articles dealing with the continuing debt problems of Brazil. What measures are being taken to bring debt burdens within manageable levels? What serious problems remain? What role has the IMF played in supporting Brazil's balance of payments and stabilizing Brazil's currency?

4. Consult recent news accounts of efforts by East Asian nations such as Thailand and Indonesia to resolve their recent economic and financial problems. To what extent have international assistance, controls on capital movements, or internal economic reforms been used to address these problems?

5. Find examples in recent newspapers of banks or nonfinancial corporations that are operating in the Eurocurrency markets. For what reasons are they borrowing or lending, and how do they appear to benefit from access to these markets?

ANSWERS TO TRUE-FALSE AND MULTIPLE CHOICE QUESTIONS

Ch.2

T/F		M.C.	
1.	F	1.	C
2.	T	2.	D
3.	F	3.	B
4.	T	4.	D
5.	T	5.	C
6.	F	6.	B
7.	T	7.	C
8.	F	8.	A
9.	F	9.	D
10.	F	10.	C

Ch.3

T/F		M.C.	
1.	T	1.	C
2.	F	2.	B
3.	T	3.	D
4.	F	4.	A
5.	F	5.	C
6.	T	6.	B
7.	F	7.	B
8.	T	8.	A
9.	F	9.	B
10.	T	10.	C

Chp.4

T/F		M.C.	
1.	T	1.	C
2.	F	2.	B
3.	F	3.	C
4.	F	4.	A
5.	T	5.	B
6.	T	6.	D
7.	F	7.	B
8.	T	8.	D
9.	F	9.	B
10.	F	10.	A

Chp.5

T/F		M.C.	
1.	T	1.	C
2.	F	2.	B
3.	F	3.	A
4.	F	4.	D
5.	F	5.	A
6.	T	6.	B
7.	T	7.	D
8.	F	8.	C
9.	T	9.	D
10.	T	10.	B

Chp.6

T/F		M.C.	
1.	T	1.	C
2.	F	2.	D
3.	T	3.	B
4.	F	4.	C
5.	F	5.	A
6.	T	6.	C
7.	T	7.	B
8.	F	8.	C
9.	T	9.	B
10.	F	10.	B

Chp.7

T/F		M.C.	
1.	T	1.	B
2.	T	2.	D
3.	F	3.	B
4.	F	4.	C
5.	T	5.	A
6.	T	6.	B
7.	F	7.	D
8.	T	8.	B
9.	T	9.	B
10.	F	10.	C

Chp.8

T/F		M.C.	
1.	T	1.	B
2.	F	2.	D
3.	T	3.	C
4.	T	4.	A
5.	T	5.	C
6.	F	6.	D
7.	F	7.	C
8.	F	8.	A
9.	T	9.	B
10.	T	10.	C

Chp.9

T/F		M.C.	
1.	T	1.	A
2.	F	2.	C
3.	T	3.	B
4.	F	4.	C
5.	T	5.	A
6.	T	6.	B
7.	F	7.	C
8.	T	8.	A
9.	T	9.	B
10.	F	10.	D

Chp.10

T/F		M.C.	
1.	T	1.	C
2.	F	2.	A
3.	F	3.	B
4.	T	4.	D
5.	F	5.	C
6.	F	6.	A
7.	T	7.	D
8.	F	8.	C
9.	F	9.	B
10.	T	10.	C

Chp.11

T/F		M.C.	
1.	T	1.	D
2.	F	2.	C
3.	T	3.	B
4.	T	4.	C
5.	T	5.	D
6.	T	6.	C
7.	T	7.	C
8.	F	8.	D
9.	F	9.	A
10.	T	10.	D

Chp.12

T/F		M.C.	
1.	F	1.	A
2.	T	2.	B
3.	F	3.	C
4.	F	4.	A
5.	T	5.	D
6.	T	6.	A
7.	T	7.	A
8.	T	8.	C
9.	F	9.	D
10.	T	10.	D

Chp.13

T/F		M.C.	
1.	F	1.	C
2.	T	2.	B
3.	F	3.	C
4.	F	4.	D
5.	F	5.	D
6.	T	6.	C
7.	T	7.	C
8.	F	8.	D
9.	F	9.	D
10.	F	10.	B

Chp.14

T/F
1. F
2. T
3. T
4. T
5. T
6. F
7. F
8. T
9. F
10. T

M.C.
1. C
2. C
3. A
4. D
5. D
6. C
7. A
8. C
9. D
10. D

Chp.15

T/F
1. T
2. F
3. T
4. F
5. T
6. T
7. F
8. F
9. T
10. F

M.C.
1. C
2. B
3. B
4. C
5. A
6. B
7. A
8. D
9. C
10. D

Chp.16

T/F
1. F
2. T
3. T
4. T
5. F
6. T
7. F
8. T
9. T
10. F

M.C.
1. B
2. C
3. D
4. B
5. C
6. B
7. A
8. D
9. C
10. B

Chp.17

T/F
1. F
2. T
3. F
4. T
5. F
6. T
7. F
8. T
9. F
10. F

M.C.
1. D
2. B
3. C
4. A
5. B
6. A
7. D
8. D
9. C
10. D

Chp.18

T/F
1. F
2. F
3. T
4. T
5. F
6. T
7. F
8. F
9. F
10. T

M.C.
1. C
2. B
3. D
4. A
5. C
6. A
7. B
8. C
9. B
10. D

SOLUTIONS TO SELECTED PROBLEMS AND SHORT ANSWER QUESTIONS

CHAPTER 2

1.

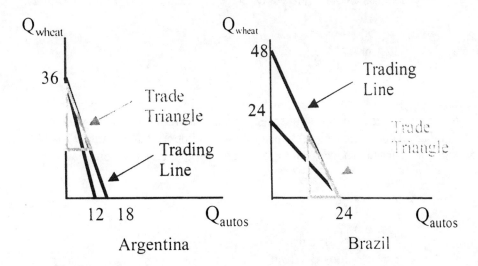

<u>Absolute advantage</u>
Wheat: Argentina (3 > 2)
Autos: Brazil   (2 > 1)

<u>Before trade</u>
In Argentina, 36W = 12A or 3W =1A
In Brazil,   24W = 24W or 1w =1A

<u>To generate trade</u>
Let 2W = 1A (between pre-trade ratios). Argentina produces and exports wheat and Brazil autos.
Potential trade triangles show 24 bushels of wheat traded for 12 autos.

2.

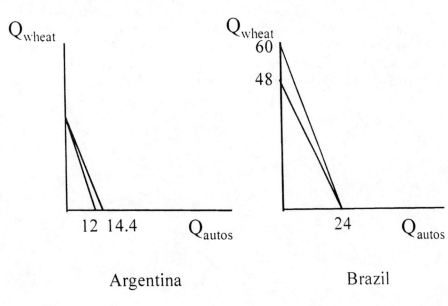

Now Brazil has the absolute advantage in both goods. But Brazil's greatest advantage is in autos (2/1 > 4/3). and Argentina has a comparative advantage in wheat (3/4 > 1/2, or 3/1 > 4/2).

Before trade
In Argentina,   36W = 12A or 6W = 2A.
In Brazil,   48W = 24A or 4W = 2A.

At a trading rate between these limits (e.g. 5W = 2A). Brazil would want to export autos (giving up 5 bushels of wheat. rather than only 4 bushels of wheat in production) and Argentina would export wheat (giving up only 5 bushels of wheat in trade to import 2 autos, rather than giving up 6 bushels of wheat in order to produce 2 autos at home). Both countries would gain.

3.   No Trade

Argentina		Brazil	
Autos	Wheat	Autos	Wheat
0	36	0	48
3	27	3	42
6	18	6	36
9	9	9	30
12	0	12	24
		15	18
		18	12
		21	6
		24	0

With Trade
Suppose 5W = 2A. If Argentina produces 36 bushels of wheat and exports 18 bushels of wheat, it could buy 7.2 autos. more than the 6 autos it could have produced along with 18 wheat. Brazil will also be able to consume 18 bushels of wheat and more than the 15 autos which it would have if it had produced these 18 bushels of wheat at home (24 autos produced minus the 7.2 autos exported leaves 16.8 autos for domestic consumption).

4.

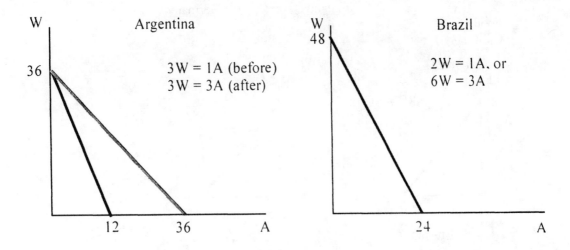

After productivity growth in Argentina's auto industry. 3W = 3A instead of 3W = 1A. Argentina now has a comparative advantage in autos. (Choose a trading price of 4W = 3A.)

5.

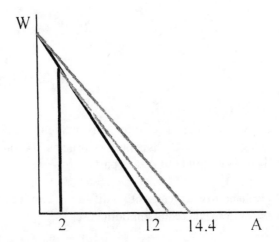

Requiring a minimum output level of 2 autos in Argentina means that fewer than 36 bushels of wheat can be produced, shifting Argentina's trading line inward (gray line).

6.

  a.   Labor per unit of output

	England	Germany
Food	6	2
Clothing	8	4

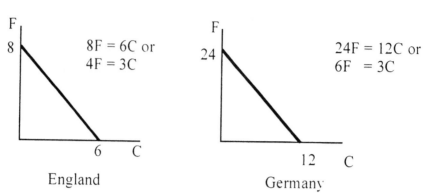

England: $8F = 6C$ or $4F = 3C$

Germany: $24F = 12C$ or $6F = 3C$

England

Germany

At $5F = 3C$, England will export clothing, and Germany will export food. (England has a comparative advantage in clothing.)

  b.   Output per worker

	England	Germany
Food	1/6	1/2
Clothing	1/8	1/4

Again, even though Germany has the absolute advantage in both products, England has a comparative advantage in clothing (1/8 is half as large as 1/4, but 1/6 is only one-third as large as 1/2). Analysis is identical to that in part a.

This pair of examples actually represents two different ways of presenting the same information, leading to identical results in both cases.

It is important to be able to work in terms of either labor per unit of output **or** output per worker. In this case, saying that in England it takes 6 workers to produce one unit of food is equivalent to saying that 1 worker can produce 1/6 unit of food.

7.

a. Production frontiers are curved or bowed out, not straight (diminishing returns, specialized resources)

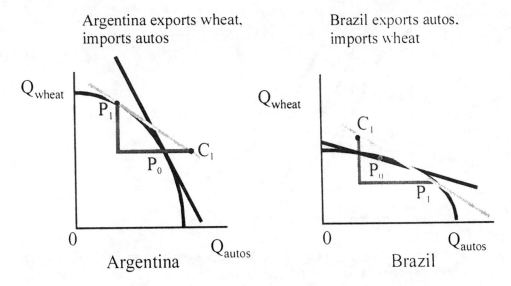

b. The slope of the line reflects the price of autos relative to the price of wheat. This slope is steeper in Argentina because the frontier shows Argentina to have a comparative advantage or greater relative ability to produce wheat.

c. Trading price lines are parallel because, with free trade, the prices or costs of wheat and autos must be the same in both countries (assuming no transport costs).

d. The line for Argentina becomes flatter (the price of wheat rises relative to the price of autos), leading firms to shift toward more wheat production (P_0 to P_1). The opposite occurs in Brazil, as the steeper line reflects rising auto prices. The trade triangles on the graphs above show possible trade; these triangles should be of equal size in order for there to be trade balance between Argentina and Brazil

8. Relative productivities can be extended to show many countries located along a spectrum from high to low productivity for individual products. This also can be done for several products rather than for only two products.

9. There has been some success in testing Ricardo's comparative advantage principle, but it is limited. The principle is valid, but productivity or production capability depends on many factors in addition to simple labor productivity.

CHAPTER 3

1.

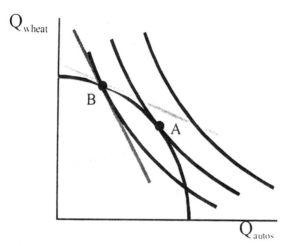

The slope of the indifference curve at point B (darker line) is much steeper than that of the production frontier (gray line), indicating that people would be willing to accept fewer autos than could actually be provided by moving from point B toward point A. At point A, the highest possible indifference curve is reached.

2.

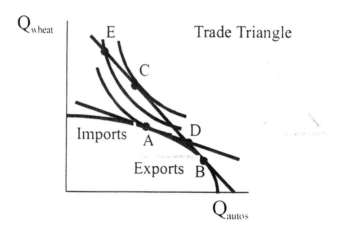

Rising auto prices (relative to wheat prices) encourage firms to shift from point A to point B in production. Consumers can now reach a higher indifference curve at point C along the trading line. Points D (along the original price line) and E also would be achievable, but consumer satisfaction would be less (lower indifference curves than at point C).

3.

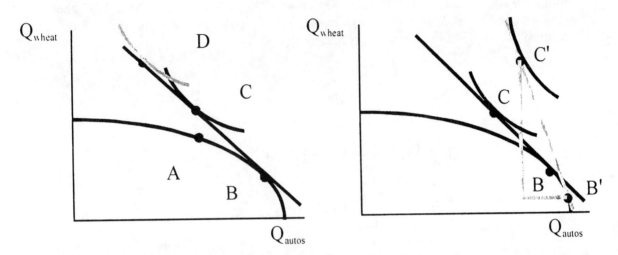

Supply (PPF frontier) and demand (indifference curve) interact to determine production point B, consumption (point C), and the trade triangle. If wheat were more preferred (gray), consumption would be at point D, and trade would be larger. With improved terms of trade (second graph), production shifts to point B ', consumption shifts to point C ', and trade expands (triangle).

4.

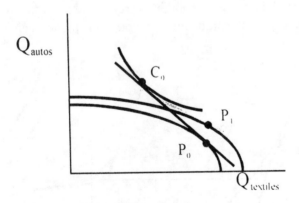

Ability to produce the traditional export product (textiles) grows more rapidly than the ability to produce autos (e.g., rapid growth of semi-skilled labor and slower growth of capital and skilled labor). The terms of trade declines (flatter budget line or trading line). In extreme circumstances, welfare may even diminish (lower indifference curve after growth): this would be "immiserizing growth" (a new consumption point C_1 would be on a lower indifference curve than the original consumption point C_0).

5.   Export prices rose by less than 10% from 1990 to 1992, and import prices rose by more than 10% (from 90 to 108), so the terms of trade declined from 1990 to 1992. From 1985 to 1992, the terms of trade improved, since $P_X = 110$ while $P_M = 108$ (base year 1985). The terms of trade also improved from 1985 to 1990, since $P_X = 102 > P_M = 90$.

$$\left(\frac{P_X}{P_M}\right)_{1985} = \frac{100}{100} \times 100 = 100$$

$$\left(\frac{P_X}{P_M}\right)_{1990} = \frac{102}{90} \times 100 = 113.33$$

$$\left(\frac{P_X}{P_M}\right)_{1992} = \frac{110}{108} \times 100 = 101.85$$

(fell from 1990 to 1992)

CHAPTER 4

1.

   a.   Mexico is relatively labor-abundant, meaning that the ratio of labor to capital is higher in Mexico than in the United States. Clothing is relatively labor intensive, meaning that the ratio of labor to capital in the production of clothing is higher than in the production of autos.

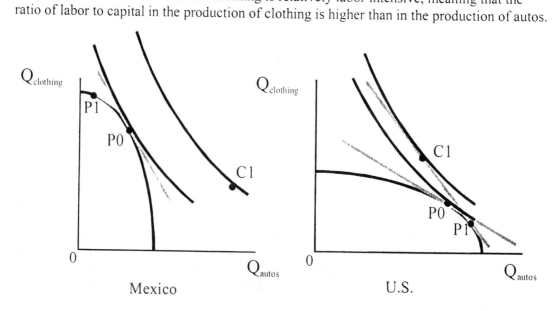

(Chapter 4 Continued)

b. Pre-trade budget line is steeper in Mexico than in the United States.
The slope of the budget line is $\Delta Q_C/\Delta Q_A$. But to move from one point to another on the budget line, total spending must remain constant. So, $\Delta Q_C \bullet P_C = \Delta Q_A \bullet P_A$. This means that $\Delta Q_C/\Delta Q_A = P_A/P_C$. Thus, the slope of the budget line also represents the price of autos relative to the price of clothing. Thus, autos are relatively expensive in Mexico (steep slope) because of capital scarcity, and cheaper in the United States because of capital abundance.

b. The international terms of trade line (which point C_1 rests on) shows P_A/P_C to be equal in both countries (free trade). $P_0 \rightarrow P_1$ as the United States shifts toward auto production, Mexico toward clothing (comparative advantage) since P_A is higher in the United States. and P_C is higher in Mexico. Trade triangles connecting P_1 and C_1 must be equal in size. If the United States triangle is larger, P_A/P_C must become flatter.
($P_A \downarrow$ or $P_C \uparrow$).

2. Wages would rise relatively in Mexico (more demand for labor intensive clothing to be produced) and fall in the United States (less scarcity of labor as clothing output falls, auto output rises). Complete wage equalization is unlikely to occur because of limitations such as trade barriers. imperfect knowledge of technology, market imperfections in United States and Mexico. or different skill levels.

CHAPTER 5

1. Use the graph to answer the following questions:

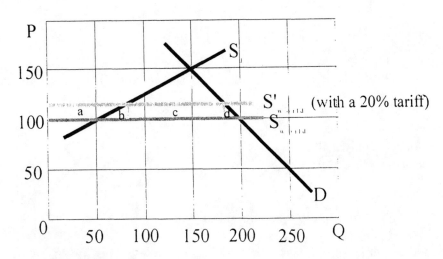

a. $P = \$150$, $Q = 150$ tons

b. Total demand = 200 tons
Domestic supply = 50 tons
Imports = 150 tons

187

c.   Total demand = 180 tons
      Domestic supply = 90 tons
      Imports = 90 tons

Total consumer surplus loss	$3800	(a + b + c + d)
Redistributive effect	$1400	(a)
Protective effect	$400	(b)
Revenue effect	$1800	(c)
Consumption effect	$200	(d)

d.   Consumer loss = a + b + c + d
      Profit gain to firms = a
      Revenue gain to government = c
      Thus, net loss to nation = b + d, which equals $600

2.

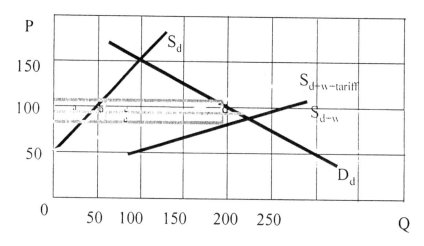

a. S_{d-w} is upward sloping, because S_{world} is upward sloping. (This country is a significant part of the world market.)

b.   Price = $90
      Domestic supply = 40 tons
      Demand = 220 tons
      Imports = 180 tons

c. $P \approx 105$, $S_d \approx 55$, $D_d \approx 195$, imports ≈ 140

d.
Total consumer surplus loss	$\approx$$3112.5	(a + b + c + d)
Redistributive effect	$712.5	(a)
Protective effect	$112.5	(b)
Domestic revenue effect	$2800	(c + e)
Terms-of-trade effect	$700	(e = 140 x 5)
Consumption effect	$187.5	(d)

(Chapter 5 Continued)

e. A country gains if e > (b + d)
In this case, e = $700 and b + d = $300, so the country gains by forcing foreign suppliers to reduce their selling price in response to the tariff.

3.

a. VA = 8/40 x 100 = 20%
EP = {[0.1 - 0.8(0)]/0.2} x 100 = 50%

	No tariff	10% tariff
Price	40	44
Materials	32	32
Value-added	8	12

(Value-added rises by 50%, from $8 to $12.)

b. EP = {[0.1 - 0.8(.05)]/0.2} x 100
= 0.06/0.2 x 100 = 30%

(Value-added now becomes $44 - 33.60 = $10.40, a 30% increase.)

c. EP = {[0.1 - 0.8(0.1)]/0.2} x 100 = 10%

When all tariff rates are the same, the effective rate of protection is simply the nominal rate.

4. An escalated tariff structure means that the nominal tariff rates are low or zero on imported raw materials and are progressively higher at subsequent stages of processing or production. This makes the effective rate of protection higher than the nominal tariff rate at each stage, creating a significant barrier for developing countries that wish to add processing to their raw materials exports.

CHAPTER 6

2.

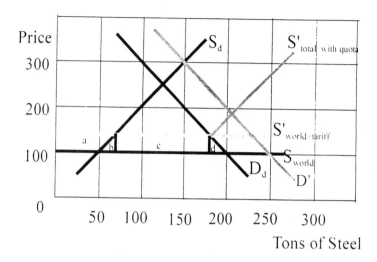

a.   Free trade: demand = 200 tons, domestic supply = 50 tons, imports = 150 tons

With a 40% tariff: P = $140, demand = 180 tons, domestic supply = 70, imports = 110.

With a quota of 110 tons, all effects will be the same except that the revenue effect probably will be lost by the country and will go to the export firms abroad.

b.   The revenue effect (area c) is approximately $4400 (110 tons, $40 per ton). Depending on bargaining strength or a government decision to "auction" quota rights, this will go to foreign export firms (setting price at $140), or to domestic import firms if they can buy at $100 and sell at $140, or to the government if it auctions or sells quota rights at $40 per ton.

c.   D shifts rightward by 50 tons at each price, to D'. With a 40 percent tariff, demand and imports both expand by 50 (D = 230 tons, imports = 160 tons). With a quota of 110 tons, supply becomes S'total with quota, and price rises to about $190, until allowable imports just meet the gap between demand and domestic supply. (Demand ≈ 205 tons and domestic supply ≈ 95 tons, so imports ≈ 110 tons).

4.	A local content requirement specifies that a certain percentage (e.g., 30%) of cars produced and sold in the United States (by United States *or* foreign firms) must consist of domestically produced cars or auto components. By increasing costs, this would raise auto prices, and perhaps would affect foreign firms more adversely than U.S. firms.

5.

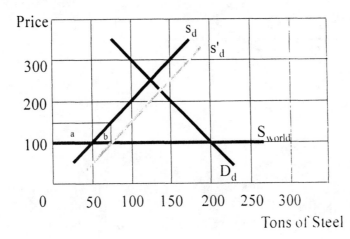

Domestic supply shifts downward by $40 at each quantity (or "outward"). Price remains at $100, demand stays at 200 tons, but domestic supply rises to 70 tons and imports are reduced to 130 tons. The loss to the nation providing the subsidy is only the protective effect (area b); the subsidy also transfers profits (area a) to domestic firms. The subsidy avoids any price distortion for consumers, compared with tariffs or quotas.

CHAPTER 7

7.

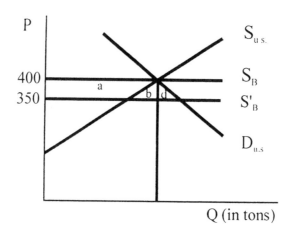

Q (in tons)

The export subsidy shifts S_B down to S'_B (at $350). Consumers gain areas a + b + d; domestic firms lose profits of area a, so the gain to the United States is areas b + d. But the United States may oppose this net "gift" for strategic reasons, or because it reduces sales of U.S. steel firms.

CHAPTER 9

2.

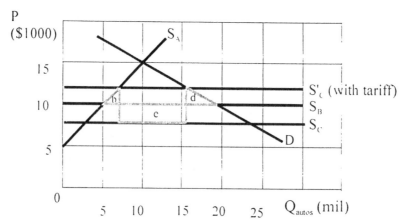

Trade diversion occurs, as Country A now buys imports from a less efficient producer than before, Country B. Cost of imports to country A rises from $8,000 per auto to $10,000. This loss, shown by area e on the graph, is greater than the net gains from the lower price to consumers, shown by areas b + d on the graph. Consumers gain as the price falls from $12,000 with the tariff to $10,000 with the union, but the trade-diversion cost is larger in this case.

3.

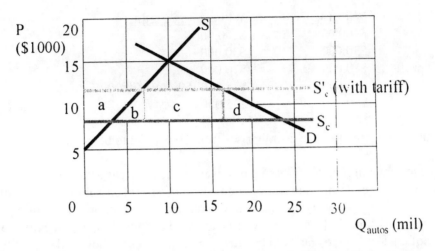

A union with country C simply expands trade with the more efficient prior trading partner. There is no trade diversion, and the net gains are now the larger triangles b and d.

4.

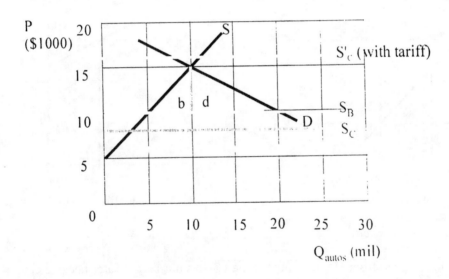

The 100 percent tariff would be prohibitive, keeping out all imports (even the price from Country C would be $16,000, above the $15,000 price at which domestic firms would supply the entire domestic market). All of the increased trade with Country B would be new trade, with net gains of areas b + d on the graph.

CHAPTER 10

5.

	With Tax Credit	Without Tax Credit
Gross Profit	$100,000	$100,000
Saudi tax	$30,000	$30,000
Repatriated profit	$70,000	$70,000
U.S. tax	$20,000 (50-30)	$35,000 (50% of $70,000)
Net profit	$50,000	$35,000

Without the tax credit, the effective tax rate rises from 50 percent to 65 percent.

6. Transfer price manipulation involves raising or lowering the prices at which intermediate products are "transferred" from a subsidiary in one country to another subsidiary in a different country in order to reduce taxes, reduce tariff payments, avoid restrictions on profit repatriation, etc. In the case of question 5, the subsidiary in Saudi Arabia would have an incentive to raise the transfer price of crude oil shipments to the United States, in order to show higher profits in the lower-tax-rate country.

8.

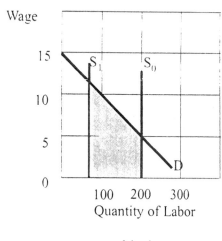

Mexico

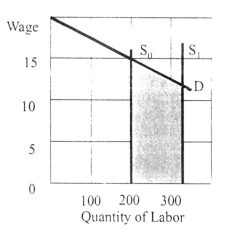

United States

Labor would migrate from Mexico to the United States until wage rates became equal. In this case, the common wage would be about $12, falling from the initial level of $15 in the United States and rising from $5 in Mexico. Approximately 120 workers would migrate. Global efficiency would improve, and output gain (shaded area under the demand for labor curve) in the United States would exceed the loss in Mexico. Free trade would alleviate these pressures for migration. Production of more labor-intensive goods in Mexico would increase demand for labor, while a shift toward more capital-intensive production would reduce labor demand in the United States.

194

CHAPTER 11

2.
a. current account, imports; debit
b. capital and financial account, long term, direct; credit
c. current account, service imports; debit
d. current account, unilateral transfers; debit
e. capital and financial account, short term; credit
f. current account, service income; credit
g. capital and financial account, long term, portfolio; debit

CHAPTER 12

2.

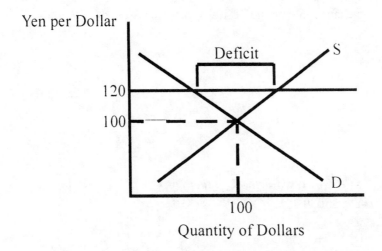

At 120 yen there is an excess supply of dollars, or a U.S. deficit. Magnitude is about 60. The equilibrium exchange rate is 100 yen per dollar. As the dollar depreciates to this level, the quantity of dollars demanded will rise as U.S. exports increase, and the quantity of dollars supplied will fall as U.S. imports decline, provided that U.S. demand for imports is elastic.

(Chapter 12 Continued)

4.   The U.S. importer would purchase euros in the forward market. This would protect the importer against a dollar depreciation. However, it also would mean foregoing any gain from a possible dollar appreciation over this 3-month period.

6.   Assuming these to be annual interest rates. the interest gain would be 2% for 180 days in the United States, and 5% in Germany. If the spot rate is 1.6 euros per dollar, the euro would be at a discount in the forward market (more euros per dollar); it would be a 3-percentage-point discount, to offset or neutralize the interest-rate differential that favors Germany. The forward rate would be about 1.647 euros per dollar. Example: $100,000 would be used to purchase 160,000 euros, which would accumulate to 168,000 euros in 180 days (5%), and convert back to $102.000 at the 1.647 forward rate (a 2% gain, just equal to what would have been realized by leaving the money in the United States).

7.   A person could exchange $1.00 for 1.6 euros, and then exchange the 1.6 euros for 128 yen (at 80 yen per mark), and finally exchange 128 yen for $1.07 (at 120 yen per dollar), thus gaining a "costless" and instantaneous seven cents (U.S.). Arbitrage would operate to eliminate this potential. A consistent exchange rate would be 120 yen = 1.6 euros, or 75 yen = 1 euro.

CHAPTER 14

3.

    a. $C = 50 + 0.8Y$

            $I = 200$

            $X = 100$

            $M = 0.05Y$

            $Y = C + I + X - M = 50 + 0.8Y + 200 + 100 - 0.05Y$

            $Y - 0.8Y + 0.05Y = 350. \ 0.25Y = 350, \ Y = 4(350)$

            $Y = 1400$

            $S = Y - C = 1400 - 1170 = 230. \ M = 0.05(1400) = 70.$

            so $S - I = X - M = 30$

b.

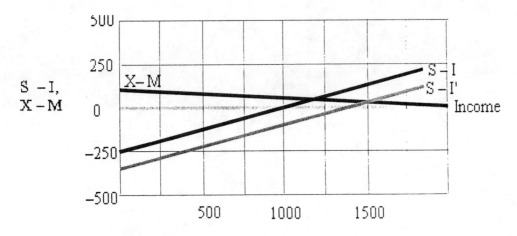

$S - I = X - M$ where $Y = 1400$
$S - I = (0.2Y - 50) - 200 = 230 - 200 = 30$
$X - M = 100 - 0.05(1400) = 100 - 70 = 30$

Or, if $S - I = X - M$, then $S + M = I + X$
$230 + 70 = 300 = 200 + 100$

c.   Multiplier = $1/0.25 = 4$
So if $I = 300$, $\Delta I = 100$ and $\Delta Y = 4(100) = 400$
or $Y = 1400 + 400 = 1800$
$S - I = 0.2(1800) - 50 - 300 = 10$

$X - M = 100 - .05(1800) = 100 - 90 = 10$
($\Delta M = 0.05$ $\Delta Y = 0.05(400) = 20$, so the trade surplus declines by 20, from 30 to 10)

d.   See $S - I' = X - M$ on graph

e.   If $\Delta X = 100$ instead of $\Delta I = 100$, there would be the same impact on income ($\Delta Y = 400$). But now, the increase in exports would raise the trade balance by 100, while the increase in income would reduce the trade balance by 20 as before, so $X - M = 200 - 90 = 110$ and $S - I = 310 - 200 = 110$. So $X - M = S - I$ as before.